BROWN TROUT HEAVEN

Brown Trout Heaven

Fly-fishing New Zealand's South Island

Zane Mirfin • Graeme Marshall
Jana Bowler • Rob Bowler

SHOAL BAY PRESS

Photo Credits

Photographs were taken by Zane Mirfin, apart from the following:
Jana Bowler (pp.40, 41, 45, 80, 108); Rob Bowler (pp.8, 43,44, 54, 109, 128, 144); John Boyles (p.126); Steve Carey (pp.35, 36); Al Davin (p.14, 46); Andrew Howe (p.77); David Lambroughton (pp.64, 75); Martin Langlands (p.83); Peter Langlands (p.18); Pete Lapidus (p.93); Georges Lenzi (pp.74, 111); Mac McGee (p.144); Leif Milling (pp.47, 98, 135, 136-7, 142); Doc Ross (p.133).

First published in 2000 by
Shoal Bay Press Ltd
Box 17661, Christchurch

ISBN 0 908704 96 8

Printed by Rainbow Print Ltd, Christchurch

CONTENTS

Nelson-Marlborough • West Coast • North Canterbury • Central South Island • Otago • Southland.

Fly rods • Reels • Leaders • Floating flylines • How to dye flylines • Subsurface flylines • Trout fly considerations for overseas anglers • Polarised glasses • Sun and insect protection • Clothing • Fishing vest and day pack • Wading equipment • Fly shops.

Aquatic insects • Terrestrial insects • Larger food items • Fly selection • Recommended general American patterns • General British and New Zealand patterns • Other recommended imitations.

Stalking trout • Reading the water • Varying stream characteristics • Spotting techniques • Blind fishing.

Dry fly fishing • Upstream nymph fishing • Strike indicators • Indicator nymphing rigs • Small wetfly fishing • Streamer fishing • Mouse plagues • Seasonal aspects of trout location and movement • Winter fishing • Fishing in adverse weather conditions • Evening fishing • Night fishing • Estuary fishing.

8. Lake and Stillwater Fishing

Find where the fish live and feed • What lake fish eat • How to catch stillwater trout.

9. Getting to the Water

Helicopters • Four-wheel-drive vehicles • Jetboats • Powerboats • Small boats • Rafting • Mountain bikes.

10. Etiquette, Expectations, Conservation

Protocol and etiquette on the water • Expectations • Conservation • Guides.

11. General Information for Visitors

Accommodation • Banking • Business hours • Currency • Driving: left hand drive • Electrical supply • Health services • Postal services • Public holidays and school holidays • Restaurants and grocery shopping • Service • Shopping for gifts • Taxes • Telephone services • Time difference • Tipping and service charges • Water supply.

Further Reading

South Island maps • Guide books • Recommended New Zealand trout fishing books • Instructional books

About the Authors

ACKNOWLEDGMENTS

Brown Trout Heaven would not have been possible without assistance and support from many of our friends and colleagues. Several have allowed us to reproduce their photographs in this book, and Claire Wallace has allowed us to use her dry fly painting to embellish the beginning of each chapter. Special thanks to Zane for the abundance of splendid photographs he provided to illustrate this book. In addition, Graeme and Zane are indebted to their spouses for their encouragement throughout the project.

Our fishing companions, guiding colleagues and Fish and Game officers have generously provided us with up to date information. We also wish to thank the many landowners who have allowed us unhindered access across their properties, the superb helicopter pilots who whisked us in and out of the back country gems we value so highly, and the owners of accommodation who catered to weary anglers after long days on the river.

Information for this book has been obtained from a number of sources. We are indebted to: R.M. McDowall, author of *New Zealand Freshwater Fishes: A Natural History and Guide* ; John Kent, author of *South Island Trout Fishing Guide*; Brian Turner, author of *The Guide to Trout Fishing in Otago*; Bryn Hammond, author of *The New Zealand Encyclopedia of Fly Fishing*; Norman Marsh, author of *Trout Stream Insects of New Zealand: How to Imitate and Use Them*; Ron Cordes and Randall Kaufmann, authors of *Lake Fishing with a Fly*; and the Southland District Fish and Game Council, publishers of *Trout Fishing in Southland New Zealand*.

Rob Bowler, Jana Bowler, Graeme Marshall and Zane Mirfin

FOREWORD

Brown Trout Heaven is the perfect title for this excellent book on fly-fishing New Zealand's South Island. As the name implies, this land of gin-clear rivers and pristine lakes has the magic allure of a piscatorial Mecca. For those anglers passionate about pursuing trout with a fly, few places on earth can rival the rich experiences New Zealand has to offer. The South Island has incredibly diverse geography from the rainforests of Fiordland to the semi-arid plains of North Canterbury. The landscape is also blessed with an amazing number of beautiful rivers inhabited by large and often wary brown trout. Like Heaven itself, these waters are not always easy for the uninitiated to discover their secrets. The following pages will provide valuable insights to unlock the treasures of this angling paradise.

Rob Bowler and I have fly-fished together off and on for over 25 years, always with a spirit of exploration and discovery. Rob's first trip to New Zealand in 1978 was planned as a sabbatical from his teaching duties at the Cate School in Carpinteria, California, where I was one of his students. In addition to his research into early New Zealand history, Rob found time to explore some of the land's famous and not so famous waters. That trip ignited a passion for the place that continues to this day. Sharing that passion are co-authors and superb Kiwi guides Zane Mirfin and Graeme Marshall. I have had the privilege to explore some of New Zealand's magical streams with both of them. Their deep knowledge of trout tactics and local stream ecology is truly impressive.

Rob and his wife Jana, Zane and Graeme have shared their vast collective experience in the pages of this book. The keys to begin unlocking the treasure of Brown Trout Heaven are contained within.

Brooks Walker III
San Francisco, California

OPPOSITE: Jana Bowler alone in a little piece of paradise. *Rob Bowler*

INTRODUCTION

Anglers dream of clear, sparkling, remote waters teeming with large aggressive trout, salmon, or their favourite saltwater fish and they are readily beguiled by stories of trophy fish, exotic locations and unique fly-fishing experiences. Indeed, as fly-fishing becomes big business and increases in popularity, remote, uncrowded, unpolluted places to fish are becoming harder and harder to find. Patagonia, Belize, British Columbia, Alaska, Norway, Christmas Island and, more recently, Russia, to name just a few places, have been the subject of magazine articles and lengthy books. But visiting such locations can be prohibitively expensive for many anglers: choices are limited by expensive accommodation, costly airfares, private water and high-priced guides.

New Zealand anglers are in the fortunate position of having world-class fishing opportunities available to them here for the minimal price of a licence fee – and South Island anglers have always known they have the best fishing waters in New Zealand. While serious anglers from other countries have been aware of the quality of New Zealand fly-fishing ever since American Zane Grey put it on the world angling map in 1926, increasing numbers of visitors from all over the world come here in search of the 'Holy Grail' of fishing, many of them making an annual pilgrimage.

The uniqueness, challenge and diversity of South Island fly-fishing will be explored within this book – possibly the first time that so much specific information about South Island fly-fishing has been contained in one volume. Directed towards anglers with previous angling experience, whether intermediate or advanced, we hope it will also benefit novices who are still serving their angling apprenticeship. We are sure it will broaden the knowlege base of the reader, whatever their level of skill and wherever they may hail from, and thus equip them with the information and skills required to have a successful time on South Island waters.

Fly-fishing should be an enriching, personally enjoyable pastime that introduces the angler to all that an area has to offer. Here the reader will be

First footprints. A place to experience beauty – and great fishing – in solitude.

OPPOSITE: Autumn in the eastern high country.

The magic of the New Zealand trout stream: clear green water, cascading waterfalls, big trout … It doesn't come any better than this for Brooks Walker.

provided with a review of the waters of the South Island – so numerous it would take several lifetimes to fish them all – and also an understanding of how to stalk and catch the large wary brown trout that inhabit these rivers and lakes.

But there is more to fly-fishing than casting and catching. A trip to the South Island will be enhanced by knowing something about geography and weather patterns, people and places, regulations and licences, entomology and trout flies, wilderness trips, travel, accommodation, guides, and conservation. This book will help to take some of the mystery, but not the mystique, out of fly-fishing New Zealand's South Island.

THE SOUTH ISLAND

New Zealand comprises two main islands, the North Island (116,000 sq.km) and the South Island (152,000 sq.km). It is about the same size as Japan or Britain. Australia, its nearest neighbour, is 1600km across the Tasman Sea. The country spans a warm to cool temperate zone from 34°S to 47°S, and is generally long and narrow, with no part being far from the sea.

It is a land of dramatic scenic contrasts. The South Island is dominated by a series of spectacular high mountain ranges that form a spine along almost the entire island. The mountains of the northern Kaikoura Ranges and Nelson Lakes National Park form the northern extremities of the Southern Alps, which continue down the West Coast and run into the steep-sided mountains of Fiordland, famous for their precipitous fiord-like sounds. Mt Cook (3754m) dominates the Southern Alps, which include about 360 glaciers. Over the past 20,000 years glaciers have carved and shaped the topography of the South Island. The West Coast is a long narrow strip of land sandwiched between the Southern Alps and the Tasman Sea.

Emerging from the jungle …
Picturesque West Coast rainforest.

The eastern side is dominated by the Canterbury Plains, formed by the merging out-wash fans from large rivers such as the Waimakariri, Rakaia, and Rangitata. High, dry plateaus dominate the central part of the island in the Otago region, and further south is the hilly, rolling country of Southland. The districts of Nelson and Marlborough to the north are blessed with sheltered river valleys divided by mountainous terrain.

The climate is generally maritime. High-pressure systems and depressions create a variable weather pattern with marked climatic differences between east and west and also north and south. Storms roll in off the Tasman Sea and hit the Southern Alps, giving the West Coast an annual rainfall that can exceed 8000mm (320 inches) and making Fiordland one of the wettest places on earth. The prevailing westerlies drop and warm as they descend from the high western ranges, creating a rain-shadow area and producing semi-arid conditions in Central Otago (300mm or 12 inches per year). Drought can be a major problem in some areas.

Fiordland, one of the wettest places on earth. *Al Davin*

Sunshine averages about 2000 hours annually. Nelson has the most, with 2350 hours; Southland the least, with about 1700. Warm, windless, clear sunny days are the best for fly-fishing, and most of the South Island enjoys its share of good weather, although heavy wind and rain can be expected at any time during spring, summer and autumn. The weather will often determine fly-fishing success.

New Zealand is among the most isolated land masses on earth, and people probably didn't find these remote islands until about the sixth or seventh century AD. The first humans were of Polynesian stock, remarkable navigators, who sailed the open Pacific Ocean in large sea-worthy outrigger canoes. They found a land dominated by a unique and varied bird life. Giant ostrich-like birds, moas, roamed the plains of the South Island until their eventual extinction; other, smaller, flightless birds fed at night in the rainforests, and large wood pigeons were easy to snare. The Maori settled throughout the country in tribal groups, creating the most complex culture of any Polynesian society. Intricate stone and wood carving characterised the artistic versatility of the early Maori people.

The weka, a native flightless bird, is an inquisitive visitor to many a South Island campsite.

The Dutch explorer Abel Tasman was the first European to discover New Zealand in 1642. But the English laid claim to the country after extensive exploration and detailed mapping by the navigator James Cook. European settlement was sparse at first. Sealers were followed by whalers, and the European population was only 2000 when New Zealand became a British colony in 1840. During the next 30 years, migration from Britain dramatically accelerated. Wars between the Maori and the English broke out; the Maori were defeated, and their culture was dramatically altered. Their population subsequently declined as European vices and diseases ran rampant.

New Zealand was thus transformed into a rather typical English colony. Many plants and animals were introduced, including cattle, sheep, deer, rabbits, possums, canada geese, and both brown and rainbow trout. Silvio Calabi, in his book *Gamefish of North America* observed that 'the British, bless 'em, did more to spread their sort of fishing and shooting than probably any other group of people on this planet. In Victorian times, and earlier, with a disregard for other fish and animal species that would be appalling in today's enlightened society, British military men, commercial travellers and fortune seekers – those who spent long periods of time away from their homeland – transplanted "their" trout, salmon, gamebirds, deer, and so on all over the planet. While assuring ourselves that we would never be so ecologically insensitive – at least now – we may heave a sigh of relief that they were, and proceed to enjoy the fruits of their labours.'

Angling solitude in the South Island high country.

Not only was the biological environment drastically modified, but the forest cover was dramatically reduced to about 25 per cent of the land area. Vast plantations of softwoods have been planted, especially *Pinus radiata*, which reaches maturity here in only 25 to 30 years. Fortunately there are still large areas of native beech and podocarp forests, especially in the national parks of the South Island.

Wild areas are still numerous on the South Island. Fiordland, Mt Aspiring, Westland, Mt Cook, Arthur's Pass, Paparoa, Nelson Lakes, Kahurangi and Abel Tasman National Parks provide residents and visitors alike with opportunities to tramp remote areas, view unique bird life, experience native forest and bush, and fly-fish remote rivers and lakes. These wild areas have been of real economic benefit to the national economy, as tourism has become the number one industry in New Zealand.

Farming is a major economic activity in New Zealand. Sheep predominate, dairy and beef cattle are numerous, deer farming is well established, and in the warmer drier areas orchards and vineyards diversify the agricultural base.

The population of modern New Zealand is about 3.8 million. North

Autumn muster on the Orari River in South Canterbury.

Islanders outnumber South Islanders by about four to one. More than 90 per cent of New Zealanders live within 40km of the coastline. Pakeha (people of white European ancestry) make up about 74 per cent, Maori 14 per cent, and Pacific Islanders 4 per cent. The rest come from many different backgrounds. New Zealanders are a proud and resourceful group of people, and visiting anglers will find them friendly, hospitable and proud to share their culture and heritage.

An excellent road network connects remote areas to urban centres. Christchurch (population 350,000) is a city of parks and gardens, located on the central east coast of the South Island in the Canterbury district. Dunedin (population 110,000), to the south, was settled extensively by immigrants from Scotland and is the capital of the Otago region. Invercargill (population 55,000) is the largest town in Southland, and Nelson (population 47,000), to the north, is a coastal town with a warm, usually settled climate during the summer months. The smaller towns of Greymouth, Westport and Hokitika are conveniently located along the rugged West Coast. All-weather, two-lane roads connect town and city centres. Driving is on the left, and roads are often narrow, but most South Island locations can be reached in two driving days.

The locals are very friendly …

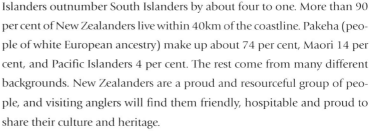

THE SOUTH ISLAND FISHERY

There were no trout in New Zealand prior to 1867. That does not mean that the many freshwater rivers and lakes were fishless; the opposite was true. The native fish fauna was varied and diverse, but there was little to interest the fly angler except a native grayling, now extinct. Large freshwater eels are still abundant in New Zealand waters, and Maori and Pakeha catch, sell and eat them. Whitebait, the young of several species of smelt-like anadromous fish, are very numerous and a delicacy. They are caught in fine mesh traps and nets.

The predominantly British colonists had a strong nostalgia for what they had left behind in England, and they imported not only many familiar plants and animals but trout as well. L.F. Aysen, the man responsible for introducing quinnat salmon to New Zealand, remarked: 'the early colonists…were much surprised to find a country with such fine rivers, lakes and streams, but with no fish with any value to them'.

Acclimatisation societies were formed throughout New Zealand to regulate the successful or, in many cases unsuccessful introduction and adaptation of exotic animals, plants and fish. Many of these exotics eventually became pests and New Zealand suffers through plagues of rabbits; farmers also curse plentiful thistles and easily spread Scottish gorse. Moose were even introduced into Fiordland but have probably died out, despite rumours to the contrary. Salmonids, (salmon, trout and char), however, were successfully planted into New Zealand waters and the modern trout fishery is made up of two predominant species, brown trout (*Salmo trutta*) and rainbow trout (*Oncorhynchus mykiss*).

Brown trout are native to Europe and have been liberated widely throughout the world. They have adapted well to the favourable environmental conditions of New Zealand; they have migrated to the sea and seeded remote rivers, especially along the west coast of the South Island. Excellent food supplies and good spawning gravels have resulted in a self-sustaining wild population.

Whitebait – a sought-after delicacy for humans and a major food source during spring for trout in many lower reaches of South Island rivers.

Brook trout (*Salvelinus fontinalis*) are a char species present in a few limited South Island locations.

Perch are resident in some South Island waters. This one came from Lake Mahinapua on the West Coast.

Tasmania was the first source of New Zealand brown trout ova. Tasmania browns were of English stock. Subsequently, different brown trout types were introduced not only from England but also from Scotland, Germany and Italy. Fifty million were released by 1916, and modern New Zealand browns are an amalgam of lake, sea-run and riverine fish introduced over the previous 130 years.

South Island browns are large. It would be difficult to give an average size, but anglers will often be casting to 1.5–2kg (3–4½lb) trout and 3kg fish are not unusual. Specimens over 15kg have been recorded and sea-run fish often reach 4–5kg or better.

A widespread adaptation to the sea seems to be one factor that contributes to the unusually large size of South Island browns. Sea-run fish reach greater size because of the abundant and varied food sources and interbreed with riverine fish. Hens that are larger can produce more eggs, and thus natural selection favours larger females. Hen fish migrate into headwater reaches to spawn and then move downstream during winter. Tagged headwater hens have been recorded in tidal estuary zones during the spring, fattening up on all that the tidal zone can provide.

In Northern Hemisphere headwaters trout are typically small. The opposite is true in New Zealand where headwater fish are often unusually large, sometimes exceeding 4.5kg (10lb). Well-oxygenated, very clear water produces large aquatic insects such as stoneflies, creepers (hellgrammites), caddis, and mayflies. Headwaters provide good habitat for these large trout morsels because water temperatures are ideal, banks are more stable, and large cobbles and bedrock mean less disruption during high water. Exceptional water clarity and quality enable trout to visually locate the available aquatic and terrestrial bugs that are necessary for large size, good condition, and fast growth. Thus headwater trout can reach trophy size, 3kg or better, but they are not usually numerous. Generally trout populations will be more numerous but with smaller average sizes in the lower and middle reaches of most rivers. Aquatic insects may be more plentiful but smaller in size as well, as the habitat can be more easily disrupted by flooding, less stable banks with more sand, siltation, and pollution from agricultural development.

Other factors that seem to influence size are the lack of disease and the general lack of natural predators. Despite the many importations, trout diseases were not widely dispersed. Hatcheries that concentrate adults and fingerlings are notoriously subject to diseases, but hatcheries are largely unnecessary, prohibitively expensive, and have decreased during the past

Martin Langlands with a beautiful sea-run brown. *Peter Langlands*

20–30 years. Predators are few and far between. Shags (fish-eating birds) are present, and large eels do prey on trout. One study indicated that the absence of eels tended to increase the numbers of trout but decrease their average size.

Browns are also diverse feeders and the South Island waters possess abundant food resources. Insects provide a mainstay diet, but browns also feed on 'bullies' and mice and in the estuaries and sea on whitebait and shoals of other baitfish. Growth rates are excellent in many rivers and lakes, and the maritime climate modifies extreme lake and river winter temperatures; growth and condition are not as adversely affected as in larger, colder continental areas.

Browns are autumn- to-early-winter spawners and survive annual spawning well. Ten- to twelve-year-old fish are not uncommon, another factor that can contribute to increased size. And of course, they live longer because browns are naturally wily. They often feed at night in deep water protected by overhanging banks and vegetation. They will feed in the shallows, however, and it is the ultimate thrill to cast to large trout rising freely to surface and subsurface insects. But they can be selective, and unsophisticated browns are a rarity even in remote locations that now can be readily accessed by hiking, four-wheel-drive vehicles and helicopters.

Rainbow trout are less abundant in the South Island than browns. Introduced in the 1880s, the original strain was a steelhead stock from the Sonoma River which flows into San Francisco Bay. They acclimatised especially well in the large lakes and rivers of the central North Island and the largest specimens of 8–10kg have been recorded there. New Zealand rainbows are notably a lake fish and are especially prevalent in the large lakes

South Island trout are often beautifully marked and coloured.

Ryan Meulemans with one of a number of fish caught one April day.

A winter rainbow.

Salmon will occasionally take a fly. A North Canterbury salmon caught on a #5wt rod before release.

east of the Southern Alps and rivers that flow in and out of these lakes. There are some large headwater rainbows in remote South Island rivers, although many famous South Island rivers have no rainbows.

Between 1869 and 1923 more than 23 million rainbow fry and fingerlings were released, and the modern New Zealand rainbow fishery is now self-sustaining and wild. Today hatchery rainbows are seldom stocked in the waters of the South Island and steelhead sea-run rainbows have not developed. As a result of all of the above, resident and visiting anglers will pursue almost exclusively browns and rainbows in the South Island.

Atlantic salmon (*Salmo salar*) were introduced into Lake Te Anau and Lake Manapouri with some short-term success; nearly three million fingerlings were liberated but did not become sea-run. The large Manapouri hydroelectric power scheme and the introduction of rainbows into this large southern catchment has accelerated the decline of the Atlantic salmon. However, there are a few still around, and the occasional fish is caught in Lake Te Anau and in Lake Gunn near the headwaters of the Eglinton River. Brook char, mackinaw and sockeye salmon were also introduced into South Island waters, but there are only a few remnant populations remaining.

Quinnat salmon (*Oncorhynchus tshawytscha*) – most commonly known in North America as chinook, or less commonly as king or spring salmon – round out the list of introduced exotic fish. The South Island is the only place where a self-supporting sea-running stock has been established outside their native rivers of North America. Quinnat salmon populate many of the South Island's east coast rivers, but a few West Coast rivers have a limited run, and escapees from Stewart Island commercial farming operations have shown up in Southland rivers.

The South Island is predominantly a brown and rainbow trout fishery. Browns are more numerous, and both species of trout can and do reach trophy size. The fly-fisher will find trout in almost all the waters of the South Island; these fish will vary in size, coloration and condition and will test the skills of all who come to catch them.

SOUTH ISLAND WATERS

The rivers, creeks, streams and lakes of the South Island are as varied as the topography and climate. Tea-coloured streams flow into the Tasman Sea from the dense vegetation of the West Coast. Clear mountain rivers emerge from the high country and fill large lakes used for huge hydroelectric projects. Glaciers cloud the headwaters of large rivers, but spring creeks stay clear after even the heaviest rain. The eastern plains are crossed by braided, unstable rivers, and smaller streams nearly dry up during hot Canterbury summer days. Back-country lakes and tarns tempt the adventurous fit angler, and huge lakes provide many kilometres of shoreline. Sea-run browns migrate up some of the larger rivers and cruise and feed in estuaries and tidal, brackish rivers. Almost all the waters of the South Island hold trout, and the angler is faced with an almost limitless variety of waters to fish.

Pristine wilderness areas and superior water clarity are hallmarks of South Island angling.

Wilderness rivers are often very rugged, presenting unique angling challenges.

The South Island is divided into six Fish and Game regions, which are administered by regionally elected Fish and Game Councils and operated by professional staff members. A fishing licence purchased in any of these regions is valid for the whole island. The cost is identical for New Zealand residents and non-residents alike. Overseas anglers should consider buying a full-season licence despite the amount of time they intend to spend fishing and should view this as a donation toward the fishery.

Angling seasons vary between regions and specific waterways, although most angling occurs between October and April. Information on the waters, the fish they contain, and regulations are available from each district or can be found in the annual South Island sportsfishing regulation publication that should be provided with your fishing licence. In some cases angler's access locations are also published and can be helpful for anglers unfamiliar with certain waterways.

NELSON – MARLBOROUGH

This region has a rich diversity of rivers, streams, and lakes. The region is known mostly for brown trout angling, with about 10 per cent of waterways holding some rainbows and the occasional quinnat salmon.

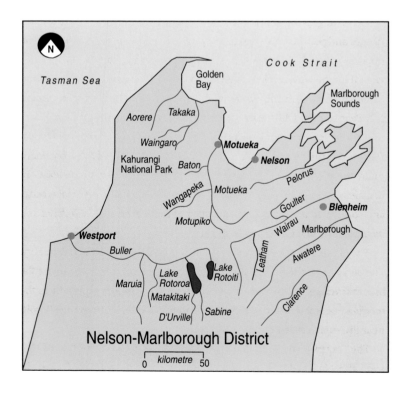

The area's rivers, rain-fed and snow-fed, often flow through orchards and farmland. Beaches, numerous vineyards in Marlborough (producing excellent wines), rugged mountains, sheltered valleys and more days of sunshine than any other South Island location are attractions that draw many visitors and anglers.

With summers usually being warm and dry, the Nelson area is more like California than any other part of the South Island. The port city of Nelson offers all the amenities the visiting angler needs and is close to excellent fishing. Other well-located bases to fish from are Motueka and Ngatimoti to the west of Nelson, St Arnaud and Murchison to the south, and Blenheim to the east.

Aimee Mirfin tries some early season fishing on the Maitai River which flows through Nelson city.

The Motueka has been called one of the best South Island rivers, a reputation earned by consistently high stocks of browns, previously recorded at approximately 200–500 fish per kilometre in some lower reaches. However, fishing in the Motueka is usually quite challenging. Good roads parallel the river for almost its entire fishable length. The river bed is stable and provides good wading. Sea-runs inhabit the lower river and periodically repopulate upper reaches and tributaries. The lower reaches of the Motueka, below the Wangapeka confluence, receive most angling pressure, as the most trout reside there.

The Wangapeka drains the eastern slopes of the Northwest Nelson Ranges and provides good angling opportunities in the lower reaches. The upper Wangapeka is remote, accessed by the Wangapeka Track, and provides the more adventurous angler with wilderness angling for larger trout.

Other significant tributaries of the Motueka are the Motupiko, Baton and Pearse, all of which offer picturesque scenery and fine angling.

Other popular angling rivers in the western zone are the coastal Riwaka Stream and the rivers of Golden Bay. Takaka hill is a formidable barrier to many travellers and has resulted in Golden Bay being one of the least visited areas in the South Island. This area has excellent fishing in tidal reaches and some wild and scenic fisheries such as the Aorere and the Takaka and its tributaries, the Cobb and Waingaro.

Two friends, two silver beards, two pipes, two fish. Dick Griffith and Hugo Melvoin with a couple of fine specimens from the Nelson/Marlborough district.

The Buller river system rivals the Motueka in popularity and quality. The best part of the main Buller is the upper 50 km above Murchison; the browns average 3–4lbs and are usually in good condition, especially in the rough-and-tumble water of the upper section as it emerges from Lake Rotoiti near the small settlement of St Arnaud.

The Travers River, which flows into Lake Rotoiti and drains part of Nelson Lakes National Park, is a wilderness stream with a good track along its

ABOVE: Late season on the upper Buller River.

RIGHT: The Pelorus river in lowland Marlborough is well stocked with browns and rainbows.

banks. The scenery is worth the walk, and well-conditioned browns popu-late the river as it makes its way across a tussock-covered valley. Also in the Nelson Lakes National Park are the D'Urville and Sabine rivers, which flow into Lake Rotoroa. The Sabine is gorgy and tumbling with good-sized browns and some rainbows. These valleys are accessible via hiking tracks and have well-maintained huts for overnight accommodation.

Lake Rotoroa, source of the mighty Gowan River as well as tributaries Sabine and D'Urville.

Flowing out of Lake Rotoroa is the Gowan River which, when it joins the Buller, doubles its flow. The Gowan is a fast white-water river where wading is difficult and dangerous but where a large population of well-conditioned trout is available to the skilful angler. Other notable tributaries of the Buller are the Owen, Mangles, Matakitaki, and Maruia, all of which are very good fisheries. The Maruia is a must visit, with high fish counts and some rainbows present above Maruia Falls.

To the east of Nelson lies the delightful Wakapuaka Stream, with good numbers of smaller brown trout. Further east, about 45 minutes from Nelson is the Pelorus River. The Pelorus has very high numbers of smaller fish, about 30 per cent being rainbows. A smaller tributary, the Rai, is wil-low-lined with a mixed fishery.

In eastern Marlborough the three major river systems are the Wairau,

Fishing the Marlborough high country.

Wilderness scenery in Nelson Lakes National Park.

Awatere and Clarence. The Wairau River and its major tributaries, the Rainbow, Goulter, Leatham, Branch and Waihopai, are popular with local and visiting anglers, and all contain some good fish in varying quantities and are very scenic. Spring Creek, which flows into the lower Wairau near Blenheim has some lovely fish present and stays clear during the heaviest rains.

The Clarence River, paralleled by a hydro road, accessible from St. Arnaud or Hanmer Springs, emerges from Lake Tennyson, and in the upper reaches holds some good-sized browns. The same hydro road also leads to the tarns at Tarndale which hold some scrappy browns. The Acheron is a major tributary of the Clarence and is well worth a cast or two.

WEST COAST

The West Coast of the South Island is a narrow and very rugged area of land marked by the northern Heaphy River and, to the south, the Cascade River. Rainfall is heavy and often torrential, as cloud masses moving eastward over the Tasman Sea encounter the mountain ranges. Many rivers are snow- and glacier-fed, prone to flooding and resulting in sparse trout populations. Nevertheless there are dozens of other rivers that clear quickly, spring creeks that are unaffected by heavy runoff, and lakes and estuaries that sustain some very large trout. Browns predominate and very few waters contain rainbows.

Apart from the fishing, the great thing about 'the coast' is the people. West Coasters are renowned for their friendliness and hospitality, and it is still possible to meet up with characters who are the South Island equivalents of Crocodile Dundee. The coast is sparsely populated by pioneer-type people and we still like to think of the area as the last frontier. Employment is dominated by the physical resources that can be harvested from the land; gold, coal, venison, timber, spagnum moss, possum skins and crayfish are important sources of revenue for West Coasters. Tourism is the latest 'gold' to be extracted from the environment.

Accommodation can be found along State Highway 6 which connects the West Coast towns of Haast, Fox Glacier, Franz Josef, Harihari, Hokitika, Greymouth and, Westport on Route 67, and Karamea.

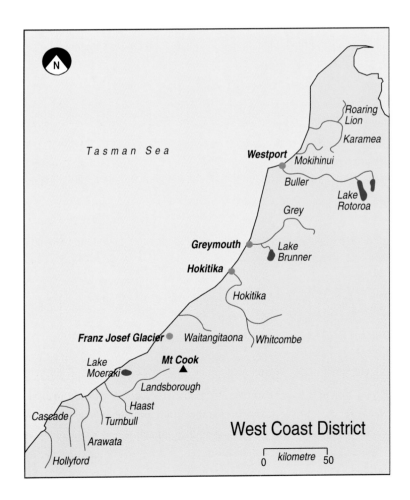

The Karamea River and its tributaries, the Ugly, Beautiful, Roaring Lion, Leslie and Crow, form the largest river system in the Kahurangi National Park, which is New Zealand's second largest national park. Except for its lower reaches the Karamea is a wilderness river accessible by walking tracks or by helicopter from Nelson, Motueka or Karamea. The Karamea and its tributaries are legendary for quality brown trout; the scenery is magnificent, providing wilderness fly-fishing at its best.

The Mokihinui is a similar wilderness river, although smaller. It has two main stems, the North and South Branches. Mokihinui fish are a discerning quarry but can be large. Be especially careful with the weather when entering such catchments; camp on elevated sites and take extra food because enormous floods are possible. We have been stuck in such locations for days in adverse weather, watching huge logs sailing downstream. On one trip we observed a flood that dammed the whole valley, where we could see only trees and brown floodwaters for days. The helicopter made several attempts to reach us before the floodwaters receded enough for a landing site to be found.

Further south the lower Buller and its tributaries, the Ohikanui, Inangahua, Waitahu, Te Wharau, and Larry's Creek provide another huge watershed for the adventurous angler. Such rivers offer some large trout that are difficult, and thus a wonderful challenge to catch.

The Grey River enters the Tasman Sea at Greymouth, and its upper reaches and tributaries provide some of the best fly-fishing on the West Coast. The upper Grey and tributaries, the Robinson and Blue Grey, offer some challenging angling, as do the Little Grey, Rough, Slatey and Moon-

The Arnold river is a premium West Coast fishery and a nationally important trout stream. This photo was taken during the summer of 1999 when the river was at an extremely low level.

light Creeks. The Ahaura and tributaries, including the Haupiri, are also well worth a look.

Lake Ianthe, South Westland, on a cool winter morning.

The Arnold River is a major tributary of the lower Grey and has its source in Lake Brunner. The Lake Brunner area has a good number of inflowing freestone streams and spring creeks; notable names include Molloy's Creek, Crooked River, Orangipuku and Bruce creeks. The Arnold River itself is a fine fishery, with daytime nymphing and evening fishing producing big tallies on occasion. If anglers have access to a boat then stillwater angling on Lake Brunner and Lake Poerua should not be neglected. As well as these, the most significant tributaries, there are many smaller streams, lakes and spring creeks that are too numerous to describe. Greymouth, Moana, Ikamatua, Reefton and Springs Junction can all be used as bases when fishing the Grey River drainage.

Driving south on State Highway 6 towards Haast Pass, there are literally hundreds of rivers, streams, estuaries and lakes that offer interesting fly-fishing opportunities. The following is a brief description of some of the best.

The upper Hokitika and the Whitcombe tributary have some rainbows, unusual for the West Coast. Duck, Harris, and Murray Creeks stay clear after heavy rains; they join the Kokatahi near the town of the same name.

La Fontaine stream is one of the more bountiful South Westland spring creeks.

The La Fontaine Stream is located near the town of Harihari and is one of the best known West Coast spring creeks.

There are possibly another dozen or so equally productive spring creeks for the adventurous angler to locate. The Waitangitaona River is spring fed and stays clear after heavy rains. Lake Moeraki and the Moeraki River hold good stocks of browns, the lake being best fished by boat or canoe. The Haast River is huge and unstable but has some notable tributaries such as the Thomas and Burke. The Okuru and Turnbull rivers are some more enticing wilderness fisheries. Further south, the Waiatoto, Arawata and Cascade rivers offer some exciting potential.

During spring and summer don't overlook fishing the tidal zones of the West Coast rivers, as sea-run browns are usually in residence and prepared to do battle.

NORTH CANTERBURY

Situated on the east coast of the South Island is the district of North Canterbury. This is the quinnat salmon capital of New Zealand. Salmon fever sweeps the area during summer, and the great trout fishing available is often neglected. Dozens of lakes make this a mecca for stillwater anglers. Six major river systems of interest to anglers are the Waiau, Hurunui, Ashley,

Waimakariri, Selwyn and Rakaia. Fish on offer include browns, rainbows, brook char, mackinaw, splake and quinnat salmon – both landlocked and anadromous.

North Canterbury lies in a rain shadow area and receives far less rain than the west coast of the island. The summer weather is dominated by dry winds that sweep over the western ranges and can produce intolerable fly-fishing conditions. Low pressure on the West Coast often means howling high winds for North Canterbury, and it is best to check the weather forecast before any excursion into the high country. The dreaded 'nor-wester' can cause windblown sediment to colour streams for weeks on end. Fortunately the Christchurch area has some pleasant fishing in more sheltered lowland rivers in such weather conditions. Rain-fed rivers can dry up during mid-summer, but high pressure systems bringing settled weather produce some excellent conditions for angling in the upper reaches of the district's rivers and in the many lakes and tarns. North Canterbury continually and consistently produces big trout for the knowledgeable angler.

Hanmer Springs is a good base for exploring the upper reaches of the Clarence and Waiau river systems. Like many of the large river systems in Canterbury the Waiau braids in its lower sections, and the upper reaches are best for trout. Waiau tributaries such as the Hope, Boyle, Nina, and Doubtful require a lot of walking but can be worth visiting.

California poppies. Streamside wildflowers abound over summer.

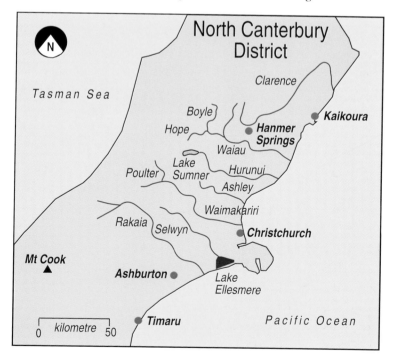

A meandering Canterbury spring creek.

The Hurunui river below Lake Sumner produces some trophy browns. Drift divers have consistently counted in excess of 50 large fish per kilometre in the gorgy stretch below Lake Sumner but be prepared for some walking and challenging wading. The area around Lake Sumner is a state forest park, and Lakes Sheppard, Taylor, Mason, Katrine and Marion all hold trout.

Lunchtime at the confluence of the Poulter and the Waimakariri.

North Canterbury rivers are often big, vast, and windswept. Beware of the nor'west wind!

The upper Ashley River can provide some good fishing throughout the season, as can the Selwyn. Two Selwyn tributaries, the Hororata and Hawkins, are good in the early season. The upper Waimakariri River and its tributaries, Poulter and Broken rivers, provide some decent fishing before the low water of mid summer. Lake Ellesmere, a huge coastal lagoon, is a prolific producer of large brown trout, mostly caught at night. Ellesmere tributaries such as the Halswell, Irwell, L2 and Hart's Creek provide angling opportunities close to Christchurch city.

North Canterbury is well known for its high country lakes, and anglers who are enticed by the challenge of large cruising trout should have a go at these lakes. South-east of Arthurs Pass National Park off Highway 73, Lakes Grasmere, Sarah, Lyndon, Pearson and Marymere vary in fishability.

The upper Rakaia provides some good trout fishing for browns and rainbows in the Lake Coleridge area. Tributaries such as the Hydra waters, Glenariffe, Ryton, Harper, Wilberforce, and also Lake Stream in the Central South Island district, provide excellent angling opportunities.

CENTRAL SOUTH ISLAND

The Central South Island Fish and Game region is a huge land area and encompasses some fine fly-fishing opportunities in large numbers of streams and lakes. In the north the region is dominated by the Ashburton and Rangitata river systems. The Rangitata and its tributaries can turn on some great trout fishing for browns and rainbows given the right conditions, especially late season. The Ashburton lakes are well regarded as superior stillwater fisheries. The upper Orari River in its gorge is very scenic and well worth a look.

Shangri-la: a Central South Island spring creek holding both browns and rainbows.

The Central South Island region is primarily dominated by the highly altered Waitaki river system which has been harnessed for a series of massive hydroelectric projects. Snow and glacier melt from the western ranges, centred on Mt Cook, flow across the high, dry plateau of the Mackenzie country and create the large Waitaki catchment. The hydro dams have decimated anadromous quinnat salmon runs, but brown and rainbow trout

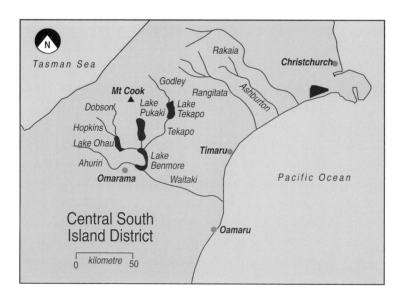

have thrived. The small towns of Tekapo, Twizel and Omarama are ideally located in the centre of this interesting region.

The premier river is the Ahuriri, which flows into the western arm of Lake Benmore. The northern or Haldon arm of Lake Benmore is larger but usually milky with glacial flows. Shallows near the mouth of the Ahuriri are well stocked with browns, and wading and stalking trout there is very much like bone fishing. The lower and middle sections of the Ahuriri are braided and in places willow-lined; high to moderate numbers of browns and rainbows are present. The upper section around Birchwood Station holds some splendid trophy browns. The prevailing wind is westerly, the residents wily, and skill and luck are essential factors. The Ben Avon and Horseshoe tarns also contain some fine cruising trout. Land-locked sockeye salmon are also common in Lake Benmore.

The lower Waitaki River is well known for its sedge hatches, especially around the town of Kurow. Lakes Aviemore and Waitaki, and other lower Waitaki tributaries are worth exploring. The Otematata River and Clear Stream flow into Lake Aviemore across a rugged, stark landscape, and the Omarama River has good evening rises on still, hot evenings. One February evening Rob's son, Ned Bowler, released fifteen browns here, some of them almost 2kg (4lb). Further down the Waitaki is the legendary Hakataramea tributary, a major salmon spawning stream that is also flush with browns and rainbows.

Just to the west of the town of Twizel, Lake Ohau, fed by the Hopkins and Dobson rivers, is a large scenic body of water with some resident fish,

The Tekapo river in late April.
Steve Carey

Mackenzie Country glory. *Steve Carey*

especially cruisers near the inflowing delta area. The Maitland and Temple streams and Huxley River are rough-and-tumble mountain tributaries, and when conditions are right, trout can be spotted in their lower pools and runs.

Lake Pukaki can similarly provide some interesting delta and spring creek fishing near the inflow of the Tasman River.

Lake Tekapo to the north of Omarama and Twizel is another large hydro lake. In the headwaters, the Godley and Macaulay tributaries hold good fish where habitat is suitable. Lake Alexandrina to the west, the Cass River and numerous small tarns are worth a trip. Below the lake, the upper Tekapo River is usually dry because of water withdrawal, but the middle and lower reaches below the confluences of the Fork Stream and the Maryburn are possibly the most productive fish factory in the South Island. The Grays River is a productive Tekapo tributary but access is somewhat difficult. The Maryburn tributary is an enticing stream worth stalking on a windless day.

The rather stark, dry character of the Central South Island district masks some remarkable and hidden fly-fishing destinations. Keen anglers should explore, seek out local information, and be patient when the wind blows.

OTAGO

The Otago Fish and Game district is possibly the most varied and diverse of all South Island fishing districts. Western Otago is mountainous, remote and very rainy. The central area is hot and dry during the summer months, similar to the high desert in the western United States. The coastal area is rolling, hilly country with moderate rainfall.

Lakes Wanaka and Hawea are located in western Otago, and many of their tributaries and feeder streams drain Mt Aspiring National Park and a rugged complex of other ranges. Lakes Wanaka and Hawea are excellent stillwater fisheries where plenty of eager fish await the observant angler. The rivers that drain into Lake Wanaka are some of the most scenic in the South Island. The small town of Hawea and the larger town of Wanaka are perfectly located for people exploring the waters of this region. When in

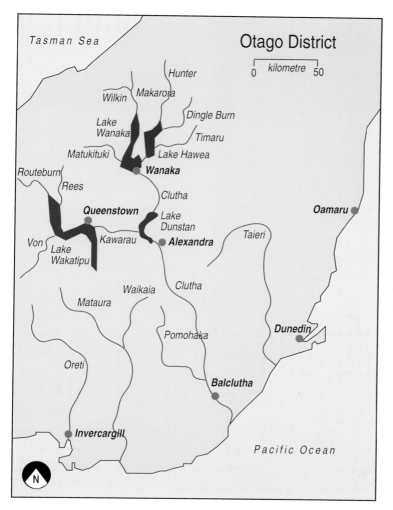

Wildflowers such as these foxgloves are a common sight in summer.

The mighty Clutha, near Lake Wanaka, is a physically impressive river with equally impressive fishing.

Wanaka don't forget to eat at Relish's Cafe on the lakefront. The food is incredible.

The Matukituki River flows into the western side of Lake Wanaka. Fly-fishing is best above the junction of the East and West branches. The East branch is often coloured by glacial silt on hot summer days, but good fishing with large dry flies can be had in this murky water during summer. Both branches are very picturesque. The village of Makarora, on the river of the same name, is the access point to visit the Young and Wilkin rivers. The Wilkin can be reached by jet boat, helicopter or walking, and the section above Kerin Forks is a fly angler's heaven. The Young rivals the Wilkin and is one of the most beautiful South Island valleys. The adventurous backpacker can tramp a loop track that connects both rivers; the scenery is spectacular. The Makarora is paralleled by State Highway 6 (the Haast Pass route to the West Coast), and Davis, Kiwi and Cameron Flats offer easy access for anglers.

The Clutha flows out of Lake Wanaka's south-east end and is the largest river in the South Island. Dive counts in the upper river show very high trout densities. Evening fishing can be electric along Dean's Bank. The Clutha is dammed at Cromwell, and the newly formed Lake Dunstan holds

high densities of browns and rainbows and looks set to become an angling goldmine as weed levels build up.

The other major lake in the area is Hawea. The Hunter River flows into the northern end. Access is by boat, aircraft or along a private road that is not open to the public except with permission from the landowners. The fly angler will find the best fishing about 15km from the mouth up to the forks of the two main branches. The Hunter is inhabited by some large browns and rainbows. Unfortunately, the prevailing wind is northerly and often blustery. The Dingle Burn enters Hawea from the northeastern shore. It is a fast-flowing, mountainous stream full of feisty rainbows. The best water is above the lower gorge, and the upper reaches are accessible from the Ahuriri Valley, tramping via a very scenic pass. Otherwise access is by boat, aircraft or private road.

The Timaru River is similar to the Dingle but more accessible and is full of spawned-out rainbows prior to Christmas. Lake Hawea is drained by the Hawea river. A very short river, it is controlled by an outlet dam, and often has good mixed trout stocks although constant flow variations and fluctuations have had an adverse effect in recent years.

The Lake Wakatipu region of Otago is famous for its resort, Queenstown.

Lake Hawea is a great fishing destination in its own right, but it is outshone by its tributaries, the Hunter, Dingle, and Timaru.

Glenorchy, near the head of the lake, and the historic mining centre of Arrowtown, to the east of the lake, also have excellent accommodation for anglers. Diamond Creek flows out of Diamond Lake and both are heavily fished but retain good stocks of trout. The Rees River is not very productive in its lower sections, but above Muddy Creek the river is clearer and more fishable. The Dart River is best left for the jetboaters but has some notable tributaries.

The Routeburn has some trophies and has now been designated catch-and-release only. The Greenstone and Caples rivers join before entering Lake Wakatipu from the northwest. Both these streams are accessible via a loop walking track, and huts are conveniently located along the tramping route. However, the beauty of these two valleys attract many eager tramper-anglers, and the browns and rainbows are usually well educated by the Christmas holiday period. The Lochy River resembles the Greenstone–Caples but access is more difficult. The Von River can be reached by boat across Lake Wakatipu or by road from the upper Oreti Valley. It is full of rainbows and is best visited in November and December because low mid-summer flows force many trout back into Lake Wakatipu.

The town of Alexandra is the best base for exploring the waters of central Otago. This area receives the least rainfall of any South Island location and is well known for its warm summers and fruit orchards. Many of the

OPPOSITE: Landing an autumn brown, Lochy River. *Jana Bowler*

BELOW: Rainbow trout heaven: the Lochy River. *Jana Bowler*

streams and rivers have been dammed for irrigation and hydroelectric schemes, forming reservoirs that have been been stocked with trout. Lake Onslow is one of the best especially during the cicada season, and can be reached from the town of Roxburgh. The Pool Burn, Upper Manor Burn reservoirs and the impoundments at Falls, Frasers, Conroys, and Butchers dams offer some fine fly-fishing for cruising trout. The climate is pleasant, and both rainbows and browns are plentiful.

Southern and coastal Otago offer some diverse opportunities. The Taieri River is big and long and varies from deep rocky gorges to meandering, swampy, slow sections. The best section for fly-fishing is the upper portion. Don't be put off by the dark peaty colour; there are some large browns in the Taieri.

Southwest of the Taieri River is the Pomahaka, a major tributary of the lower Clutha. The Pomahaka offers more than 50km of varied angling, and brown trout from 1kg (2lb) to 6kg (14lb) inhabit its waters. The upper section flows through hilly, windswept country, and resident browns mix with sea-run fish to produce some trophy angling. The water is clear, and ripples and runs separate deep pools. The upper Pomahaka is a real challenge and the big browns are steelhead-strong. Try this section after rain, just as it clears. The sea-run browns are moving then and not schooled up in the deep pools.

There are many more South Otago streams, too numerous to mention. The best of the lot, the Waipahi River, is a major tributary of the lower Pomahaka. Its catchment has been extensively modified by conversion of native tussock into pasture, but it still holds good stocks of feisty browns.

The Waikaia River, the major tributary of Southland's famous Mataura River, rounds out the varied list of Otago waters. The Waikaia's source is in the Umbrella Mountains and is best fished from where it emerges from beech forest around Piano Flat to its confluence with the Mataura.

SOUTHLAND

The Southland fish and Game district covers about 15 per cent of the land area of the South Island and comprises both Fiordland and Southland itself. Southland is a region of rolling farmland with a few mountains in its northern portion and generally flat in the south. Invercargill, on the south coast, is the largest town. There are four major Southland river systems: the Waiau, the Aparima, the Oreti, and the Mataura.

The Waiau originates in Lake Te Anau, the South Island's largest lake, and also drains Lake Manapouri. The Waiau's flow has been drastically

reduced by the huge Manapouri hydroelectric project, which diverts most of the massive flow from the Waiau via tunnels through turbines into the sea at Deep Cove, Fiordland.

Rob Bowler in amongst the golden tussock of the Mavora Lakes.

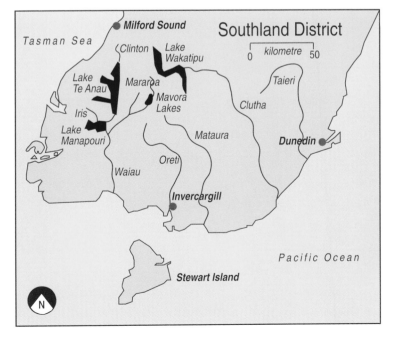

Tussock-lined Upper Mararoa. *Rob Bowler*

Tributaries of the lower Waiau worth mentioning are the Lill Burn, paralleled by the road to Lake Hauroko; the Wairaki, a braided inaccessible stream; the Borland, bush-lined, with spectacular scenery; the Monowai Stream, difficult to fish because of its very bushy banks; and the Orauea, a lovely pastoral stream. The upper Waiau, which carries the full flow from Lake Te Anau into Lake Manapouri, has prolific insect life and its rainbows can provide some memorable battles. It is best fished at lower flows when gravel beaches are exposed in the upper reaches or by boat.

The flow from two of the Waiau's major tributaries, the Mararoa and Whitestone, is also diverted. The weir at the juction of the Mararoa and Waiau Rivers blocked passage of spawning and sea-run trout, but a state-of-the-art 'vertical slot fishway', unique to New Zealand, has been installed, a project completed with the co-operation of Meridian Energy and the Southland Fish and Game Council. Sea-run, resident spawning browns and rainbows are now returning to the middle and upper reaches of the Mararoa, enhancing an already good fishery.

The Mararoa is one of Southland's best rivers. The upper section flows through a stark, tussock-covered valley and is accessed by 4WD vehicle or by boat across the North Mavora Lake. The middle reaches are bouldery and can be difficult to wade, even in moderate flows, and the lower section is gorgy and harder to reach. Both rainbows and browns are residents, with many fish over 3kg (6½lb). The North and South Mavora Lakes also have excellent mixed populations of trout. The Whitestone, a major tributary of the Mararoa, can also provide the angler with some good sport and the occasional large trout. Rain fed, it can dry up before it reaches the Mararoa and is best fished early season.

There is a huge backwater on the Mararoa River. *Rob Bowler*

The Aparima, tree-lined and flowing in a southerly direction, has a good population of moderately sized brown trout, with often spectacular evening rises. The Hamilton Burn joins the upper Aparima and is one of its major tributaries.

The Oreti River provides the fly-fisher with more than 100km of brown trout water. The upper reaches are easily accessible, and the trout, although big, are spooky and hard to catch, especially when the persistent north-westerly wind makes fly-fishing nearly impossible. The middle reaches are more braided but trout populations are higher, and the lower section produces some large fish for spin and bait anglers, with fish in excess of 12kg (26lb) on record.

The Mataura River is the second largest Southland river and one of the most famous and productive rivers in the South Island. Its source is in the Garvie and Eyre mountains, south of Lake Wakatipu. It flows in a south-easterly direction across gently rolling farm country, turns south at Gore, and meets the sea near Fortrose. The phrase 'mad Mataura rise' has been

Mac McGee with the seventh fish from one pool in the middle reaches of the Mataura. *Jana Bowler*

Headwaters produce large browns and beautiful rainbows. *Al Davin*

often used to describe the prolific insect life and rising trout that inhabit the Mataura, and when conditions are right 'the rise' can be magnificent.

The upper Mataura is paralleled by State Highway 6, but below Parawa the river cuts through a roadless, hilly section known as the Nokomai Gorge and emerges again at Cattle Flat, an area dotted with small holiday houses. The middle reaches hold excellent populations of brown trout, and the lower section below Gore and Mataura is known for bigger trout. The predominant insects are caddis and mayfly, and hatches often occur in the early to mid-morning hours and just at dusk, especially when the weather is warm. The Mataura is a delight to fish and numerous backwaters hold large cruising fish. Rain can dirty the river quickly and it clears slowly, especially in the middle and lower reaches. The Waikaia, the largest tributary, tends to clear faster, and smaller Mataura tributaries such as the Otamita and Waimea are well worth visiting when the main Mataura is unfishable.

Most of the Fiordland region of the Southland Fish and Game district is encompassed in Fiordland National Park, the largest national park in New Zealand. This World Heritage Park is rugged and heavily forested and has annual rainfall of more than 7500mm in places. There is an incredible variety of fly-fishing water, much of it accessible only by foot or boat, as helicopter access is restricted in many areas. Some remote Fiordland rivers are virtually unfished and contain trophy trout. Adequate preparation must be made before a Fiordland trip, and caution must always dictate plans, as heavy rains can cause rivers to rise to fearsome levels very quickly.

The tributaries of Te Anau are numerous and some are more easily fished than others. The Clinton River enters the northern end of Lake Te Anau and is accessible by boat and paralleled by the famous Milford Track for most of its length. The Clinton is a beautiful bush- and tree-lined river; big browns and rainbows can be seen from the track and are a real challenge to catch. The Clinton, like all Fiordland rivers, rises quickly and clears just as quickly. The Worsley rivals the Clinton as a quality fly-fishing experience and there is always a chance for big trout. The Worsley is characterised by rugged terrain, difficult access and sandflies the size of fantails.

Other tributaries flowing into the western side of Lake Te Anau are worth exploring. The Glaisnock and Lugar Burn enter the north arm, the Doon flows into the middle arm, and the Ettrick Burn empties into the lake near the Te Anau glow-worm caves. All these rivers hold browns and rainbows but the Clinton and Worsley are the easiest to wade and fish.

The Eglinton River flows into and out of Lakes Fergus and Gunn and enters the east side of Lake Te Anau. Fergus and Gunn hold a few Atlantic

Chasing cruising rainbows on the North Arm of Lake Te Anau. *Leif Milling*

Catching South Island brownies is an electrifying experience for Chuck Foster.

salmon as well as rainbows and browns. The Eglinton is one of the most scenic rivers in the world and access is easy from Highway 94 (the Milford road) to its grass- and tussock-covered banks. The Upukerora River rounds out the list of significant Lake Te Anau tributaries and is a major spawning stream, which is best fished early season.

Lake Manapouri, although only half the size of Te Anau, is still a very large body of water. The major tributaries of this beautiful lake are the Grebe, Iris Burn, Spey, and Freeman Burn. The Spey and Iris Burn are best. Don't ignore the possibility of cruising fish on calm mornings along the lake edge.

Numerous Fiordland rivers flow directly west into the sea. Most of these rivers are virtually inaccessible and can only be reached by long arduous hikes or very expensive helicopter flights. We have been eyeing up these rivers for years on maps, fantasising about potential exploration, but have been so busy exploring the rest of the South Island that we might have to wait a few more years before we get to dangle a line in all of them. Without doubt, this area is the last great Holy Grail of South Island trout fishing. If you do venture into these rivers, you will be braving all that Fiordland can dish out.

For less hardy souls, the Hollyford and Cleddau rivers off the Milford road and the Arthur River accessible from the Milford Track are a little easier to reach.

EQUIPMENT AND CLOTHING

Good equipment is essential to be consistently successful when fly-fishing the South Island. Camouflage, comfort and performance are prime considerations.

FLY RODS

Despite advances in technology, casting performance still depends on the angler, but good equipment can turn an intermediate angler into a high achiever. Without a doubt, the Americans lead the world in fly rod design and manufacture, although some New Zealand brands are satisfactory for many situations.

Most South Island fishing will be done with 5-6 weight outfits. Lighter rods (3–4 weights) are useful in smaller streams or when more delicate presentations are required. Heavier outfits such as 7–8 weights are useful in larger rivers and are especially good for lobbing heavy nymph rigs. Most anglers prefer longer rods, 275–305cm (9–10 feet), because of their superior casting performance. This is essential for blind fishing or casting into wind as more line velocity can be achieved. Three- or four-piece pack rods are very handy in New Zealand for backpacking and helicopter trips; they cast nearly as well as two-piece rods but are more easily transported on aircraft.

Some favourite fly-fishing rigs (from top to bottom):

Sage SSP 890-3 with Islander No. 2 reel and #WF8 line;

Sage LL 486-3 with Orvis Battenkill 3/4 disc reel and #WF4 line;

Sage RPL 590-4 with Ross Reel Gunnison G-2 reel and #WF6 line;

Loomis IMX9', #6, 4 piece with Loop Dry Fly reel and #WF7 line.

REELS

Most reel brands are very good these days. They should hold at least 100m (328 feet) of backing and need to have a smooth adjustable drag. Reels with an exposed outside rim are ideal for putting additional pressure on.

LEADERS

South Island trout fishing often requires long leaders to avoid scaring trout with flashing and splashing floating fly-lines. The major exceptions are fishing sinking fly-lines when a deep fly presentation is required, fishing after dark, or throwing large wind-resistant flies. Tapered leaders are essential to transmit the energy of casting, progressively and accurately, from the fly-line to the fly.

During the day it is an advantage to use a leader of 3–5m (10–16 feet) in length. If the fish are exceptionally wary and the angler can handle such leaders, they can stretch as long as 6m (20 feet). Such long leaders require relatively good casting skills to turn over, and a tailwind is an advantage for any angler.

Long leaders help to present the fly to wary fish, keeping the fly-line flash, silhouette and splash to a minimum. Such leaders are better for blind fishing too, because the trout are less likely to see the fly-line float over them. Longer leaders also allow anglers to position the fly further ahead of a fish without scaring it with the fly-line. This is especially important when a fish is lying in deeper water because a nymph will take longer to sink to the desired level.

Many companies produce some good unknotted leaders designed for varying circumstances. For New Zealand conditions, however, many commercial leaders are too finely tapered and will not perform well in wind or in turning over heavy, wind-resistant flies, as they are prone to twisting and tangling when used with larger flies. Although South Island fish are sometimes tippet shy, a longer leader with a relatively heavy tippet is often required to best present the fly. Shop-bought leaders should be tapered to

---

HAND-TIED LEADER FORMULAE

The best leader designs that we've found are the work of South Westland guiding guru Dave Heine of Greymouth.

Dave Heine – Short Leader

Length (cm):	63	63	56	56	46	46	46
Diameter (mm):	.57	.55	.50	.42	.37	.30	.22 + tippet
Breaking strain (kg)	17	16	12.5	10	7	4.5	2.7

Dave Heine – Long Leader

Length (cm):	76	76	61	61	56	45	45	45
Diameter (mm):	.60	.57	.55	.50	.42	.37	.30	.22+ tippet
Breaking strain (kg):	18	17	16	12.5	10	7	4.5	2.7

These designs have worked for us, but experimentation may be necessary to find leaders that suit your fishing style and specific fishing situations.

1–3x so you can add your own intermediate section before tying on an appropriate tippet.

Consider tying your own leaders for best performance and economy. Tie the leader butt sections with Maxima (ultra-green) and Mason nylon brands, which are stiff and ideal for New Zealand fly-fishing conditions. Blood knots are good in the upper sections and, contrary to the opinions of many anglers, will not bounce apart if they are tied properly.

Tippet nylon is usually a softer, more flexible brand of nylon to allow the best presentation. As fish have become more wary, lighter tippet strengths are preferable in many areas. Drennan and Umpqua are favourites because of their fine diameter-to-strength ratios. However, in rivers with less sophisticated trout, Maxima is great for its high abrasion resistance, especially in rough-and-tumble mountain streams. It is also an excellent choice for streamer fishing. Always use some form of lubrication such as saliva when tying knots, and never tighten them too fast as you can easily damage the tippet material.

Most brands of nylon are good and have differing qualities that can be selected by the angler for different purposes. Always use fresh nylon if possible and never allow your nylon or fishing vest to be exposed to insect repellent, sun or excessive heat.

Leader glitter can be lessened with a new tippet by running it through sand or gravel, or a commercial preparation can be used. It's easy to manufacture your own leadersink formula to minimise reflected flash and casting surface shadows by mixing equal quantities of fuller's earth and glycerine.

Remember that New Zealand trout are often big, tough fish living in a rough environment that can seriously abrade your nylon. Always test or frequently retie your terminal knots and replace tippets after hooking a few fish.

FLOATING FLY-LINES

Floating fly-lines are the most commonly used lines in the South Island, and many companies produce a good-quality product. Anglers should consider using one line weight heavier than recommended to load their rod. Using a slightly heavier line helps in many circumstances – wind, short casts, long leaders, casting heavy nymphs, and so on.

Colour is an important factor in line choice. Most guides and knowledgable local anglers will refuse to fish with bright-coloured fly-lines, especially the horrific fluoro colours. Many companies are now making grey/olive/brown lines for New Zealand conditions, and overseas anglers

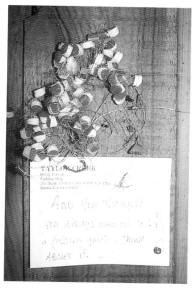

Fly fishing consumes lots of nylon and sundry equipment, especially when you're guiding!

are now recognising the usefulness of these colours on their own homewaters.

Dull-coloured lines flash less and are better camouflaged against the sky, trees and water. Such lines will definitely allow the skilled angler to hook more fish. They are also better for blind fishing, as they can float over a fish without disturbing it.

Anglers often argue that they need a bright line so they can control and see the line more effectively. This idea is flawed, as you should be watching the fish or your strike indicator. If a line is too camouflaged it may be difficult for less experienced anglers to gauge what length they are casting, but they will soon learn to gauge line length instinctively and hook many more trout than with their super-visible fly-line.

How To Dye Fly-lines

If your lines are too bright they can be easily dyed to a suitable colour. The best dye in New Zealand for such purposes is called Dylon, which is available in chemist stores and some supermarkets and hardware stores. Favourite combinations include Jungle Green, Desert Dust and Coffee Colour.

Follow the mixing directions, heat the combination to boiling, and take off the heat. Place the first 5m of line in the mixture, stir around with a stick until the desired colour is reached, then remove and dunk in a bucket of cold water. Let it soak for a few minutes, remove and wipe dry with a rag. When the mixture cools you can store it in a screw-top bottle for next time.

It doesn't pay to dye the full flyline, as dying can affect the line coating, which may disrupt casting and hinder shooting line through the line guides of your rod.

SUBSURFACE FLY-LINES

Although most South Island trout fishing is undertaken with floating lines, some sub-surface lines are very handy for certain circumstances and techniques and give the angler more options under varying conditions. Among the most useful are:

Clear slow sinking intermediate lines

These are great for fishing stillwaters and lakes, as they present no surface wake and are not subject to surface interference by waves and wind. These lines are described more thoroughly later in the book, in the section on stillwater fishing.

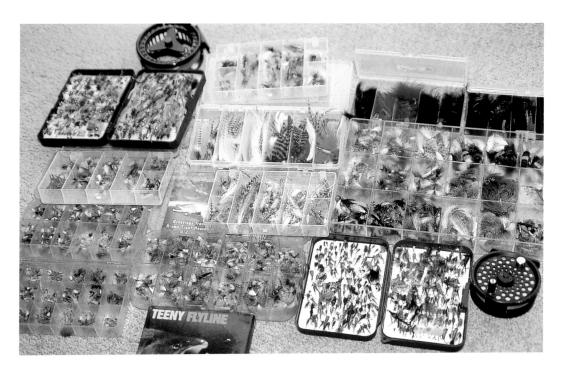

Sinktip lines

These come in a range of sinking densities and lengths. Particularly recommended are the Scientific anglers 4m (13ft) sinktips in III and IV class sink rates for rivers and lakes.

Airflo Poly Tips

These new lines are also very handy. These mini-sinking tips, 3m long, attach by a loop system to your floating line. They range in sink rate from intermediate through to super-fast sink. Such sinktips cast well, are inexpensive and are easy to store in vest pockets for specialist fishing situations.

Shooting heads

It's hard to beat Teeny fly-lines, which are made in a wide range of weights measured in grams. The larger Teeny lines need a heavier rod such as an 8 weight to throw them and can also be useful for harling behind a boat. Probably the most useful New Zealand sizes are T130, T200, T250 and T300. Such lines can put your flies on the bottom fast.

TROUT FLY CONSIDERATIONS FOR OVERSEAS ANGLERS

New Zealand, American and British fly patterns are widely available in New Zealand sporting goods stores and are of generally high quality. If

Which fly? The eternal angling question!

A fine fish, but the angler is in danger of a painful case of sunburn. Sun protection is a must.

your plans involve extensive use of New Zealand guides, they will usually carry a wide range of flies suitable for specific locations and you will therefore not need to bring as many flies. The New Zealand Customs Department will not allow *natural* fly-tying materials (feather, hair, etc.) to be brought into the country, though artificial materials will cause no problems. Commercially tied flies will be allowed by customs officials, but home-tied flies or fly-tying materials may have to be fumigated on arrival.

Overseas anglers should respect New Zealand Customs procedures to limit risks to our valuable agricultural industry, which is free of contamination by foreign diseases and viruses. Visiting anglers should be especially careful to cleanse waders and especially wading boots by bleaching to remove any chance of disease being spread. Pack them in the top of bags for inspection by customs officials. Camping equipment should be sanitised, and tent pegs sterilised by boiling.

POLARISED GLASSES

Polarised glasses are essential. Good-quality lenses will protect your eyes and put more fish in the net.

SUN AND INSECT PROTECTION

Sunscreen and lip protection are needed most days. New Zealand has one of the highest rates of skin cancer in the world because of the lack of pollution and the bright clear atmosphere. South Island sun has the ability to blister and burn without tanning.

Insects are a problem in some areas. Mosquitoes and particularly sandflies can be fierce, and some anglers develop severe swelling after being bitten if they are inadequately prepared. New Zealand sandfly stories are rife, but remember they help to protect the fish from anglers in backcountry regions! Some of the best fishing is when the sandflies are at their worst. Usually if there are no sandflies around, the fish aren't as active either.

Be sure to cover up well and use plenty of insect repellent. The sandflies can be vicious! *Rob Bowler*

New Zealand insect repellent is best because it was developed on New Zealand insects. Brands such as Repel, Rid and Dimp are good. Also recommended are scarves and light-weight mesh or bonefish gloves to stop sunburn and insect attack.

Many areas of the South Island have a wasp problem in late summer, and numbers can build up to plague proportions. Watch where you step and be careful grabbing onto trees as you may encounter wasps. If you feel a sharp sting, run away to avoid more.

CLOTHING

Warm clothing in dull colours (includes rain jacket and visored hat) are best for fishing. Camouflage patterns, dark greens and khaki, are ideal for stalking wary brown trout.

FISHING VEST AND DAY PACK

Equip your vest with all the usual items: leader material, flies, clippers, fly floatant, scissors, forceps, sunscreen, bug repellent, split shot, etc. A day pack (a small backpack) is valuable for carrying lunch and snacks, rain gear and extra warm clothing.

WADING EQUIPMENT

Waders

Lightweight stocking-foot waders are probably the best compromise – walking even moderate distances in neoprene is like walking around in a sauna. Lightweight waders are compact and fit in luggage and are good for early and late season, inclement weather, and blind fishing big rivers. Gore-tex waders 'breathe' well, remove perspiration buildup and are excellent for New Zealand fishing conditions. Barbed-wire fences, prickly gorse, and spiky matagouri bushes can wreak havoc on lightweight waders, so it pays to be careful around such obstacles.

Hayden Thompson exposes as little skin as possible as he takes a midday siesta in sandfly country.

Boots, wading shoes

South Island fly-fishing can often involve lots of walking. Anglers often wear a pair of sturdy hiking boots and wade wet in shorts. Felt-soled wading boots and gravel guards are a good compromise for wading and walking, but are very slippery on grass. We often use carbide-studded wading boots on slippery rivers, especially in bouldery type streams on the West Coast and Fiordland, the only disadvantage being the noise transmitted through the stream bed.

Wading wet

Full-length nylon wading pants or polypropylene long underwear and nylon running shorts are the best all-around gear for mobility and comfort. The 'polypro' long underwear can keep the sun and sandflies from causing damage, it dries quickly and keeps you warm. Try wearing long nylon, wool or cotton pants over the polypro underwear in late summer for extra safety from potential wasp stings. Wear sturdy wading or high-top walking

The jacket is not a great colour for serious trout stalking – but Campbell Whyte seems to be in luck anyway!

A well-stocked fly store.

shoes and possibly two pairs of socks. Always take polypropylene or woollen clothing to keep your upper body warm as well, even in the summer.

Most of the time, wading wet is best but flexibility is the key. The day might be cold to start with, so light-weight waders are appropriate. If it warms up, take them off and carry them in your day pack. Wade wet or switch to polypropylene long underwear with your light-weight shorts if the sandflies are numerous.

FLY SHOPS

Most towns in the South Island have at least one store that sells fly-fishing equipment. The equipment is much more available in New Zealand than in years past, but the cost is still quite high compared with pieces of similar items in other countries.

ENTOMOLOGY AND IMITATIONS

 It is worth knowing something about South Island entomology and there are some useful books listed in the bibliography which will give more detailed information than is possible here. This very brief description is intended to provide a review of the aquatic and terrestrial insects that make up the diet of most New Zealand trout. We also wish to describe some alternative trout food sources not commonly imitated or mentioned in other South Island fishing publications.

AQUATIC INSECTS

There are many dozens of New Zealand aquatic species in the diet of New Zealand trout. The caddis and mayfly group are predominant during most of the fly-fishing season. Caddis, both cased and uncased, are numerous and co-exist with mayfly nymphs in most streams and rivers. The most common forms are horn, stick and free-living caddis.

New Zealand has numerous mayfly species, which undergo remarkable changes from nymph to adult. Many artificial patterns have been devised to imitate these cyclical stages – nymph to dun to spinner – and the angler's box should be well stocked with different sizes, colours and weights to take advantage of periodic trout feeding binges.

Mayfly nymph.

Stoneflies are prolific in fast-flowing bouldery rivers and vary from bright olive to brown and black. They are a large insect, slow moving and clumsy in flight as adults. We often use stonefly nymph patterns after a fresh, as the water clears and levels fall. Although present throughout the fishing season the best time to fish with artificial stonefly nymphs is in spring and early summer.

At the adult stage Dobson flies or creepers (hellgramites) are somewhat similar to stoneflies. The creeper larva has pincer claws and stout forelegs, with a buff-coloured abdomen and grey legs. Big trout love to gobble creeper nymphs.

Other aquatic life of interest are waterboatmen or corixae, back-

Representative caddis patterns which work well.

Brian Roeske samples the aquatic insect population of the upper Buller River.

swimmers, midge pupa, damselflies, dragonflies, aquatic snails and craneflies. Corixae are present in most stillwaters, ponds, lake margins and backwaters. Midge pupae, commonly known as bloodworms, inhabit muddy-silty areas along stream sides and stillwaters and, after pupation, rise to the surface in large numbers. Snails are present and available to trout, mostly in stillwaters.

Damselflies and dragonflies are usually taken by trout during nymphal stages but occasionally an adult imitation will be taken by trout. They are mostly stillwater dwellers inhabiting weed beds and other debris. Adult craneflies look like a large mosquito and occur in a variety of sizes. The larval cranefly looks like a big maggot.

All of these aquatic insects are significant parts of the angling equation, although caddis and mayflies contribute most to the trout main menu.

TERRESTRIAL INSECTS

Terrestrial insects are very important to South Island trout, especially during warmer months when they provide a summer feeding bonanza for hungry fish. Terrestrials are often larger than aquatic insects and can become available in large quantities. They are extremely important to trout in many relatively infertile South Island streams, and anglers should always be on the lookout for a terrestrial feeding frenzy.

Beetles are very prevalent along most rivers and lakes. Black beetles in varying sizes are very numerous, especially near areas of native bush. Brown beetles are a common evening phenomenon around many lowland waterways during mid-summer. Probably the best-known beetle is the green manuka beetle, which is usually abundant during November and December. The green beetle has an iridescent green wingcase, and trout feeding on manuka beetles can be suckers for a well-presented imitation.

The willow grub is a terrestrial larva that often becomes available to fish from mid-summer onwards. The grub emerges from a reddish blister, which blights waterside willow trees. During emergences hundreds can fall into the water, and trout rise to feed on these pale yellow black-headed worms. The willow grub is difficult to imitate, not so much in its colour and shape but rather in its twitching, squirming motion. Anglers should try twitching subsurface or even slightly weighted imitations in front of fish to obtain best results.

In mid- to late summer between January and early March, the cicada is king. A large olive insect renowned for its high-pitched chirping, the cicada often appears in large numbers. This season is the time that large

Brown trout can be suckers for a well-presented terrestrial pattern, in this case a black cricket.

trout lose some of their caution and feed ravenously, much to the delight of the dry fly purist. There is nothing like a trophy trout rising to a cicada pattern. We have seen many expert anglers turn into blathering idiots with 'buck fever' when huge browns cruise up and inhale a #6 dry fly.

Other terrestrial insects on which trout feed include black ants, black bush insects, blowflies, bluebottles and leaf-hoppers. Large New Zealand native insects such as wetas, cockroaches, bush beetles and smaller thrips can also be seasonally and regionally significant.

Weta, a native terrestrial insect, with suitable imitations.

LARGER FOOD ITEMS

Trout will virtually eat anything that finds its way onto or into the water. Large trout require large amounts of food to maintain their body condition and growth. The following food sources can really work trout into a frenzy.

Large earthworms are prime trout food and imitations can be expected to produce on many lowland streams and high-country waters where there are eroding earth banks.

Small fish food sources include bullies, smelt, inanga, whitebait, mullet, small trout and eels. Such forage fish are eagerly sought and make a nutritious and tasty meal for predatory trout.

Crustacea such as koura (freshwater crayfish) are regionally significant in many waters. Shine a spotlight into many streams and it can be amazing how many koura are out prowling nocturnally. Other crustacea such as shrimp and crabs can be important in estuarine trout diets.

Amphibians, both immature tadpoles and mature frogs, are eaten by trout. Rodents such as mice and rats can be seasonally important, helping some big trout to grow even bigger. We found up to 12 mice in the stomach of one 3kg trout.

Late-season trout foods such as salmon eggs, trout eggs and rotten flesh may also be worth imitating.

Remember that trout are adaptable fish and will eat whatever food sources are available at the time.

FLY SELECTION

Most trout flies will work if they are presented to the fish at the right level of the water column, and anglers should use whichever flies they feel most confident with. As fishing pressure increases and trout become more discerning, it often pays to use a more exact imitation. Many trout have become selective, and imitations most closely representing the shape, size and colour of the preferred naturals will be the most successful.

The mighty Stimulator, an excellent summer dry fly.

Some favourite American dry flies (clockwise from 3o'clock): Parachute Adams, Parachute Caddis, Royal Wulff, H&L Variant, Irresistible, Humpy. Centre: Adams.

Here we list patterns that are often used to imitate each major food source. No fly is *guaranteed* to succeed, but many proven specialist patterns outperform general or attractor patterns. We also like to use flies different from the average angler's because trout in commonly fished waterways are starting to recognise and reject, and even bolt for cover when presented with hare and copper nymphs, royal wulffs, etc.

RECOMMENDED GENERAL AMERICAN PATTERNS

Dry flies: Adams #10-22, Adams Parachute #10-16, Cahills, Hendrickson, Quill Gordon #12-18, Elkhair caddis #6-18, Comparaduns and no-hackles #12-18, Royal Wulff #10-16, H&L variant #8-12, Humpy (green, red, black) #10-14, Bivisible (brown and black) #6-10, Stimulator (olive) #6-10, Daves Hopper #6-8, Umpqua Cicada #8-10.

Nymphs: American Pheasant Tail #10-20, Teeny nymph #12-16, Zug Bug #10-14, Lambroughton Flashback #10-14, Rubberlegs (various) #4-10, Beadheads #8-16, Brassie #12-18.

Streamers: Krystal and Woolly Buggers (black, olive, brown, white, blood) #4-12, Muddler Minnow #6-8, Olive Matuka #6-10, Zonkers #6-8, Clouser Deep Minnows #6-10.

GENERAL BRITISH AND NEW ZEALAND PATTERNS

Dry flies: Kakahi Queen, Twilight Beauty, Cochy Bondhu, Dad's Favourite, Molefly, Red Tipped Governor, Black Gnat, Greenwells Glory in various sizes.

Some very useful dry flies (three columns, left to right):
1. Dad's Favourite, Kakahi Queen, Cochy Bondhu
2. Greenwell's Glory, American Thorax dry, Adams, Black Gnat
3. Blue Dun, Twilight Beauty, Black Wulff, Red Tipped Governor

Nymphs: Hare and Copper #8-16, Buller Caddis #10, Nelson Brown #10-12, Green Stonefly #6-12, Halfback #10-14.

Streamers: Grey Ghost, Taupo smelt flies, Canterbury streamers, etc., Hairy Dog, Fuzzy Wuzzy, Hobnailed Boot, Matukas, Hamills Killer, Craigs Nighttime, Mrs Simpson, etc., sizes #4-10.

OTHER RECOMMENDED IMITATIONS

These are a few of our own personal favourites:

Rob Bowler: Cicada

Body: Green, black, brown or pale yellow dubbing. Brown hackle over dubbing, tied Palmer style.

Wing: Thick bunch of stacked elk or deer hair, tied thick and down along sides, with head trimmed somewhat rounded.

Comment: Rob's Cicada looks similar to a large elk-hair caddis although it has a much more chubby appearance. A great fly during mid-summer. Floats well on #6–8 hooks.

The Rob Bowler Cicada, a prime South Island summer fly.

Steve Carey: Tekapo Terminator

Hook: #12–16.

Rib: Fine wire.

Tail: Pheasant tail fibres.

Body: Pheasant tail.

Trout anglers aren't the only fishers along the edge of a river …

Thorax: Hare fur.

Wingcase: Pheasant tail.

Wings: Cul de Canard tied spent.

Comment: Steve's spent spinner is a pheasant tail nymph with wings. Deadly when trout are on spent spinners or feeding near the surface.

Zane Mirfin: Horn Caddis

Hook: TMC 2457 #12–16.

Rib: Dark copper wire.

Body: Yellow/olive floss silk tied curved and tapered from hook bend to head.

Thorax: Hare fur guard hairs tied sparse.

Comment: Nothing new with this pattern – there are plenty of other versions that work just as well. The floss silk should go a brownish olive when wet. It is a good idea to have a variety of colours and weights to suit different rivers. It is especially useful on lowland waters. If they won't take this you're in trouble …

Zane Mirfin: Green Tungsten Caddis

Hook: Kamasan B175 #10-16

Bead: Black tungsten 5/32, 1/8, 3/32

Thread: Black

Weight: Lead wire, if additional weight is required

Rib: Dark copper wire

Tail: Black whisks

A selection of Zane's favourite imitations: Green Tungsten Caddis, BTH Attractor, Horn Caddis.

Body: Bright green dubbing

Thorax: Peacock herl

Legs: Black krystal flash

Comment: Used on its own or in tandem as a sinker nymph. Catches anything that swims. Just add water …

Zane Mirfin: BTH Atttractor

Hook: Kamasan B175

Bead: Copper metal bead or tungsten for heavier models

Thread: Brown/black

Tail: Black whisks

Weight: Lead wire, if additional weight is required

Rib: Dark copper wire

Body: Peacock herl

Thorax: Claret seal fur or synthetic

Hackle: Grizzly hackle dyed purple, tied sparse

Comment: Useful nymph in many situations.

Ian Cole: Damsel nymph

Hook: Tiemco TMC3761 #10-16

Tail: Dyed olive partridge breast

Abdomen: Fine olive dubbing

Rib: Gold or green wire

Thorax: Dubbed olive squirrel

Wing case: Turkey

Comment: This versatile fly is the complete stillwater all-rounder, representing damsels, mayflies, small bullies and midge.

Ian Cole: Black & Peacock

Hook: Sprite sproat nymph hook #12-16

Body: Twisted peacock herl, tied plumpish

Hackle: Two turns black hen hackle

Comment: A particularly valuable stillwater fly when dressed in an array of sizes, suggesting a submerged beetle, diving beetle or corixa.

Peter Carty: Carty's Green Stonefly Nymph

Hook: TMC200R #6-8-10

Thread: Green

Peter Carty: guide and fly-tier supreme.

The classic creations of Peter Carty. The general terrestrial and stonefly patterns should be an essential item in every fly box.

David Lambroughton Cadillac Nymphs: a great South Island nymph pattern. *David Lambroughton*

Tail: Green goose [biots]

Underbody: Lead wire #6 030, 8 025, 10 020

Abdomen: Tan/olive dubbing blend

Rib: Medium olive vinyl

Thorax: Olive dubbing

Wing pads & case: Olive/green nylon fabric used for tents, umbrellas, etc.

Legs: Olive dyed soft hackle eg. Hamill's Killer feathers

Antennae: Orange accent flash

Peter Carty: Carty's GT (General Terrestrial)

Hook: TMC200R #6,8,10

Thread: 1/0 orange

Body: Fly foam, yellow, green, black

Body hackle: Brown or black saddle hackle

Underwing: Pearl accent flash

Wing: Shimazake fly wing , medium grey #02

Head: Whitetail deer hair, natural, green, black

Sighter: Brightly coloured egg yarn, red or green

Legs: Black rubber legs, medium or small to suit fly size

Peter Carty's General Terrestrial, a very effective summer dry fly.

STALKING TROUT

To many visiting anglers the concept of stalking and spotting a trout before casting to it has something of an air of mystery and even sorcery about it. It is a process that, quite rightly, has captured the imagination of thousands of anglers. Les Hill and Graeme Marshall (one of the authors of this book) should take some credit for raising awareness of the technique in their aptly named 1985 book *Stalking Trout*, in which they brought together much existing knowledge and related it to their own experiences and observations over a considerable timespan. *Stalking Trout* was an awfully long time in the making, requiring much planning, theorising and most importantly, practical application. If the actual writing was sometimes onerous, the thrill of putting ideas into practice was certainly not. For some years the business of stalking large trout was almost an obsession. The authors of this book are still addicted, but have that addiction under control (to some degree) and now enjoy other forms of angling almost as much.

The truth of the matter is that sight fishing is not new. It was a technique commonly employed on the English chalk streams centuries ago and of course is *de rigueur* when fishing for bonefish on the tropical sand flats. In New Zealand the practice has been largely confined to back-country North Island streams, but is arguably more suited to South Island waters, especially the bush streams of Nelson, Westland and Fiordland. But when conditions are right the stalking technique may be employed with confidence on the big, brawling rivers of Canterbury and Otago and with equal success on the middle and lower reaches of rivers like the elegant Motueka or lower Pelorus. Conversely, even in this country of clear, unpolluted rivers and streams, some waters are just not suitable candidates for the technique. When conditions are right, however, sight fishing, or 'stalking' can be deadly.

Many Kiwi anglers have known this for a long time, and although initially the preserve of a relatively small band of highly skilled and somewhat

Classic sight fishing produces a hook-up on a beautiful South Island morning.

Crystal-clear water makes for exciting sight fishing.

secretive nymph fishers the method is employed by dry fly anglers too. Arguably the first to popularise the technique in this country was Tony Orman in his 1974 book, *Trout with Nymph*. While Tony's book was primarily about nymph fishing techniques, perhaps its most interesting facet was the pursuit of browns in shallow water. Stalking and successfully inducing a take from a large brown trout is one of angling's greatest challenges. Parts of the Motueka River are ideally suited to this technique, especially when the water is clearing after a fresh, or conversely when the fish are nymphing heavily in very shallow, riffly water.

The first American Graeme introduced to the stalking method reacted quite strangely. Graeme had been asked to look after a friend of a friend for a few days, a keen trout fisher and deer hunter. Even though Jim was a little overweight he seemed reasonably fit, so off they set into the wilds of north-west Nelson, loaded down with camping gear, rods and a rifle. They never got to use the rifle, but the rods had quite a workout. En route to a favourite stretch on the river on the first day Graeme began to explain that conditions were perfect for spotting and that they would be looking for individual fish. Jim's rejoinder staggered him. 'But that's un-sporting. It doesn't give the fish a chance!' Graeme tactfully tried to explain that in this river there were quite low numbers of fish and that to achieve any hook-ups they had to search out each individual. Blind fishing would probably get them onto a few, but would also mean a great deal of effort for mediocre results.

Jim just shook his head in disbelief and fell in behind Graeme on the bush track winding through the cathedral-like beech forest. Soon they scrambled down the dinner-table-sized rocks to the water's edge. The day was perfect. Wraiths of mist still clung to the olive-hued slopes but the patches of blue increased in size by the minute. Graeme could hardly contain his excitement. Even though he carried a rod he was determined that his guest should strike the first blow. He rigged him up with a long leader, tapered down to a 3x tippet, with a well-weighted hare and copper nymph on the business end. A metre and a half up the leader he tied on a piece of bright orange wool indicator and dipped it in liquid fly floatant. Like a setter on the hunt Graeme moved straight into stalking mode, searching methodically among the angular rocks for any sign of a fish. The stream sucked and gurgled around the exposed boulders which dotted the run. With polaroids and a wide-brimmed hat the conditions were well nigh perfect. Jim sauntered along behind, fishing methodically all the tiny little pockets, which Graeme didn't have the heart to tell him were fishless. Too

Prime pools with good structure will almost always hold good fish.

The elusive prey.

small in the main to hold anything bigger than a 15cm fish, he had none-theless given them a quick glance. Miracles sometimes happen.

Graeme hadn't gone 20 metres before he spotted one, predictably, right in the pocket between two large, submerged boulders. This fish was really on the go, feeding at will on the smorgasbord of nymphs coming down the feedline. As he hunkered down and watched, the fish continued to feed, never deviating more than a metre from the centre of the food-pro-ducing sluice.

'I've got one here, Jim,' he called to his companion. 'Come on over and have a go at it.' Disbelief was written all over Jim's face, but he did as he was told. Graeme pointed out the whereabouts of the fish in relation to other landmarks. 'Nah, I don't see any fish,' Jim muttered, and try as he might Graeme simply could not get him to see it.

'Okay, then, I'll tell you where to cast.' Graeme soon had him in posi-tion behind the fish and pointed out exactly where the nymph should go. The first cast went off to the right, but the fish continued to feed. Graeme breathed a sigh of relief and urged Jim to try again, just a little to the left. He still had an incredibly disbelieving look on his face, but he was polite enough to do Graeme's bidding.

'Perfect!' Graeme shouted. 'It's after it – STRIKE!' The guide almost fell off his rocky perch as Jim whipped the rod tip up. Jim felt the solid resist-ance but was totally unprepared for what happened next. As he described it later, a 'submarine' came out of the water.

The rest is history. Somehow Graeme's 'Doubting Thomas' companion subdued a large, wild brown, more by good luck than good management. It turned out to be a typical fish for the river about 2.5kg (5lb) and 60cm (24inches) in length – far and away the biggest trout of any species Jim had ever landed. It was admired and photographed for longer than was probably healthy for the fish and then returned to the river. The hand-shaking and back-slapping went on for some time, along with the usual 'Gol-darns' and 'I'll be damneds.' Graeme was definitely 'flavour of the month', and there was no further talk of unsporting behaviour.

Jim had a ball that day with a number of fish up to 3.5kg in the net. But not one did he see, even after they had been spotted for him.

In retrospect Graeme came to the conclusion that part of the problem was the fact that he looked *at* rather than *into* the water. It is also possible that anglers attempting to spot fish for the first time expect to see the entire fish in glorious technicolour. Little do they realise that even the very best of Kiwi anglers see little more than a hint of a fish in most situations.

Corner pools with stable structure offer the best opportunities in braided alluvial eastern waterways.

Upstream sight fishing on a small beech-lined stream.

Indeed, situations where the entire fish is visible are rare and mainly re-stricted to the clearest of back-country streams on the most perfect of days – and normally from an elevated position.

It needs to be made clear that sight fishing is not the panacea for all ills. It is simply another part of the thinking fly-fisher's armament. Many kiwi anglers have been tempted to think that if they couldn't spot a fish there probably wasn't one there. But most professional fly-fishing guides, who encounter every weather and water condition that this fair land of ours can produce, now realise that if one were not prepared to utilise blind fishing techniques, very few fish indeed would be hooked. Sight fishing is some-thing they attempt on virtually every outing, but is not the be all and end all – rather it serves to add the spice that makes fishing in New Zealand the superb challenge that it is.

There is a myth abroad that Kiwi anglers are blessed with some form of extrasensory perception, which enables them to find fish visually at will. Oh, that it were true! Like most skills, expertise comes the hard way – by doing it at every possible opportunity. Anglers gain that expertise by devot-ing many hours of misspent youth fishing when they probably should have been concentrating on their studies. They don't have the eyesight of Superman. Zane Mirfin and Graeme Marshall have developed a hunter's

Outside curves on rivers often offer some fine trout habitat.

Even a tiny stream like this one could hold some very large trout.

eye for things wild. Both dedicated hunters, they frequently astonish others with their ability to spot game at great distances or in poor light, such as picking out a hare or rabbit hunkered down in the far corner of a field as they drive along the highway. A deer-hunting friend of Graeme's was always astonished by his ability to find deer on the open tops at great distances without binoculars. Keen observers of nature, whether hunters or not, make the best spotters of trout.

Spotting trout is a learned skill, and one that any reasonably observant angler can learn. Some fish are obvious to everyone with average sight. Those tantalising beasts that hover just under the surface of some huge, calm pool overshadowed by towering beech trees are not difficult to see, but with rare exceptions such fish are also virtually uncatchable. No, the fish we are interested in are to be found mainly in much shallower water, where they rely on their natural camouflage and nearby boltholes to survive. The fact is that much of the best food is to be found in shallow water. Unlike their North American brethren, New Zealand brown trout are just as apt to feed on tiny mayfly nymphs in bright sunlight as they are on small fish, koura or other large food items. That is where we must target them. Even experienced anglers never cease to be amazed at some of the locations in which they find big browns. While rainbows are more inclined to feed mid-stream in the fast, oxygenated water, browns are often comfort lovers, expending as little energy as possible while keeping body and soul together. They rely on their astonishing ability to adapt to the prevailing natural coloration of the streambed.

READING THE WATER

If there is one skill essential to spotting trout it is the ability to eliminate low-probability water. Most skilled anglers do so instinctively if spotting fish is the primary objective. We frequently limit our searching to quite small parts of the stream, leaving the water that's more difficult to see into for blind fishing. While space does not allow for a detailed niche-by-niche description of favoured trout lies, it is worth outlining the main parts of a stream identified by Les Hill and Graeme Marshall in *Stalking Trout*. These niches were isolated by extensive observation and meticulous recording over a number of years.

The Eye of a Pool

This is the prime feeding position. The real hot spot of the eye is right alongside the 'seam' or line of current delineation. Feeding fish will lie in the quiet water to the side and sidle over into the fast water to intercept passing food items. If danger threatens they will quickly disappear into the fast water. This position is a superb one, as it gives the fish the opportunity to have first go at food entering the top of the pool, yet rest when not actually feeding. If there is a prominent rock present in the eye there will almost certainly be a fish on the upstream side of it. This location does present drag problems, however, surely the fly-fisher's worst enemy. To some degree drag can be lessened, if not eliminated, by positioning oneself in direct line astern of the feeding fish, or on the edge of the current in the laminar flow as much as possible.

In Front of a Rock

In much fishing literature anglers are exhorted to target the area behind an outcrop or rock. Such advice does not stand scrutiny. If one observes the area immediately behind such a feature it will be obvious that a rotor effect is operating, causing considerable disturbance of smaller particles of sand, etc. Besides, the trout cannot see and line up its prey. By contrast the upstream side of a rock has a comfort zone caused by the backwash off the structure that is virtually motionless. Just as importantly, the fish can see its food coming. Most of our back-country waters have boulder-studded runs. It pays to peruse the upstream side of each prominent obstruction carefully.

Downstream of a rock

While trout rarely linger long immediately below a rock for the reasons outlined above, the position some metres downstream is a different pro-position altogether, especially when another rock a little further downstream

Large boulders and difficult terrain characterise many wilderness streams, but the additional challenge is part of their attraction.

ABOVE: Obstructions in the water, such as this fallen tree, can provide prime feeding lies for trout.

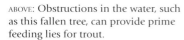

RIGHT: Even an overhung, grassy bank deserves careful inspection.

affords yet another comfort zone. This, of course, is why pocket water is often so productive. Those who pass it by without the respect it deserves do so to their own detriment.

The lee of a bank obstruction or extension

While this is a relatively minor niche it is certainly important in the total scheme of things and may form the only calm stretch in a long area of turbulent water. Browns, especially, love such a place, particularly if it also provides a snag or overhanging bank to retreat to. The extension need not be particularly large or significant to provide an area where the current is slowed just enough. One stretch of the Maruia River comes to mind in this regard, especially when flowing swiftly after rain. The bank extensions are little more than chunks of grassy bank that have slumped into the river, but they so frequently harbour a fish that they need very careful inspection.

There are many minor niches, and those that are occupied only occasionally. The Motueka produces an interesting phenomenon at times when there is a very heavy hatch of the *Deleatidium vernale* mayfly, with fish feeding across very shallow riffles running diagonally across the stream. While these fish seem to throw caution to the wind they are often extremely difficult to spot. On sunny days they often give themselves away by the shadow they cast on the bottom. These grey ghosts provide superb sport on #16 and #18 pheasant tail or similar nymphs. Really good feeding binges of this type simply don't occur frequently enough for us.

VARYING STREAM CHARACTERISTICS

Throughout the South Island streams vary enormously, and it is worth examining the special characteristics of the main types likely to be encountered. Even within one region stream topography demonstrates enormous variability. The Nelson–Marlborough area with which the writers are so familiar could easily encapsulate the South Island in microcosm, as it possesses examples of virtually every type of water likely to be encountered.

The Motueka River is one of the best-stocked brown trout streams in the country, but one could be forgiven for thinking otherwise at times. The trout are well fed and fickle in the extreme, feeding only when it suits them. The main fishing areas are the relatively gentle, long runs, where the best areas to target are at the top of the runs and where variations in flow occur. This freestone river features all the feeding niches mentioned above, though rock outcrops and obstructions are less in evidence than in its tributary feeder streams. The stalking angler will not find fish occupying any specific water type to the exclusion of others, and they may be found very close to the shore at times. Stalking and spotting on such a wide, open river requires very good visibility and is best attempted when the sun is

Endless riffles on the Motueka provide ideal trout habitat and plentiful angling opportunities.

high overhead and the sky cloudless. This type of river is best fished using a combination of spotting and blind fishing techniques. Frequently it is best to fish it blind entirely, or target rising fish. It is important to target high-probability areas for the closest scrutiny, as outlined above.

Motueka fish can be moody and respond best when significant hatches are occurring, although they can quite inexplicably turn off when the air is full of mayflies. Such problems serve only to intensify our determination to solve them.

By contrast, the Buller is an example of a much more robust freestone river. At times quite braided where it flows through rough grasslands in its upper reaches it is important to target the more stable areas. Relatively deep, fast-flowing runs are worth careful scrutiny, with the eye at the top of each pool providing sanctuary for some big, strong fish. Classic pocket water occurs where the river is more stable. The niches above and between large rocks are often the most productive. Look lively when a big Buller brownie takes off, as it may seem determined to reach the Tasman Sea without delay.

A true alluvial river is typified by the Wairau. Unstable and braided for long distances it is similar to many Canterbury rivers. Despite the basic instability such rivers harbour some large browns. Wherever structure in the form of permanent rock is to be found, there will be fish. In the lee of

The alluvial rivers of the Omarama area offer fine sight fishing for both brown and rainbow trout. *Georges Lenzi*

bank extensions is a prime spot. Although there is often much walking involved between fish the effort can be very worthwhile. The upper reaches of some of these rivers provide superb pocket fishing where larger boulders stud the bottom. In Canterbury small side streams meandering through the tussock sometimes harbour large fish which use the overhanging banks to provide cover.

Nelson's Riwaka is not a true spring creek, but with one branch issuing from a cave system it clears quickly and supports excellent insect populations. The fish are often large and exceedingly wary in such clear streams, but they can be caught using long, fine leaders and small flies. Search the eye of each pool carefully and look for fish positioned under the willows and long grasses trailing into the stream.

Perhaps the best known spring creek system is the La Fontaine on the West Coast. Here look for fish feeding off the edge of weed beds in the fast-flowing and exceedingly clear water. Nowhere is a stealthy approach more important than in this type of stream. Once disturbed these fine specimens simply disappear into the weeds and under the overhangs.

The magic of a West Coast spring creek. The dense weedbeds offer plenty of food and security for resident fish. Such streams often stay clear after heavy rainfall.
David Lambroughton

SPOTTING TECHNIQUES

Sight fishing for trout has become something of a trademark of South Island fishing, especially away from slow-flowing lowland regions. On the best days it can provide memories which will linger for years afterwards. Even on days of wind and rain, sight fishing can produce astonishing results on the right waters. More about that later.

The ideal day for sight fishing is cloudless with only the gentlest of upstream breezes blowing. Pigs might fly! While the South Island provides many days of this type, we can and do experience the worst weather imaginable at times – days on which most anglers would simply forsake the river for more comfortable pursuits. Some, though, see such days as a challenge, and some of the best days in terms of fish hooked and landed have indeed been atrocious weather-wise.

On such a day on the Motueka River a year or two ago Graeme was guiding two US anglers who were proving to be quite difficult clients. One had landed three magnificent fish on a back-country stream the previous day, all of them spotted by Graeme before a cast was made. One took the net scales down to a little under 4kg (8½lb). But these characters remained hard to please, and when the next day broke to reveal angry grey clouds, wind and rain, the mood was far from cheerful. Graeme knew that all the rivers would be rising quickly with the heavy rain, so he chose to fish very close to their accommodation.

The clients expertly cast double nymph rigs into a very slightly coloured Motueka. The fishing was slow – surprising really, as a rising Motueka is often really 'hot'. Try as he might Graeme couldn't spot anything close in. The river was just so wide and featureless that the surface simply glared back at him. All the same Graeme encouraged and cajoled his rather grumpy clients, and eventually they succeeded in landing a fish of about a kilogram each, but this didn't improve their mood. The rain set in even harder, and the anglers became aware of water trickling down their necks despite the excellent wet-weather gear they were wearing. By late morning the river began to rise appreciably and was soon on the verge of being unfishable. Graeme was just about to announce a retreat when he decided, purely on a hunch, to investigate a small side channel flowing against tall willows. By now it was considerably larger than usual and had formed a large shallow pool. A fair volume of water was flowing through.

As Graeme approached from the lower end he saw that the water was still quite clear, with the bottom clearly visible despite the pounding rain. He also noted with interest that the backdrop of trees provided a glare-free surface. Suddenly his heart skipped a beat as out of the corner of his eye he sensed rather than saw the tiniest dimple on the surface. Was it just a raindrop? On full alert now he watched closely, and there it was – a fine brown

Is that a fish? Actually this American couple never saw the trout they caught until it had attached itself to their line.

trout finning quietly in less than 30cm of water. Looking further upstream he was rewarded with the beautiful sight of no fewer than seven fish, for all the world like peas out of a pod. Cautiously backing off he approached his clients and presented them with the good news. With trembling hands he removed their nymph rigs, added some 5x tippet and tied on #18 parachute Adams dries. Acutely aware that something as insignificant as a dislodged rock could give the game away they moved into position.

At first Graeme thought the fish had gone, but as his eyes became accustomed to the gloom there they were. All were feeding avidly on nymphs, but just occasionally they would suck in a dry with such delicacy that the rise could hardly be distinguished from the fat raindrops. Not a single fish could be seen by Graeme's clients, but they knew from his demeanour that he wasn't joking.

John was first up, and he made no mistake about placing the fly right on the nail. There was little doubt about the take as the fly was sucked in with relish, a pause and then the water turned to foam as the fish felt the hook. The 2kg brown just wanted out, and presumably went the way it had come as it zoomed downstream and out into the main river, by now a roiling, muddy torrent. It was quickly subdued, netted and released. Al was next, and he also made no mistake with cast or strike. The clients were smiling now. Each in turn took three fish out of that miniscule pond. Every fish took off downstream as if stung by a wasp and was landed on the edge of the main current. The last fish finally realised that all was not well and vacated the premises unhindered. Before the flood-waters really came down the anglers raced off to another similar spot and succeeded in fooling three more fish before the conditions became impossible.

This little example serves to emphasise just how much sight fishing techniques can save your day.

While the ideal spotting conditions have been outlined above, there are significant exceptions that should be considered. Both early and late in the season back-country streams become quite difficult to see into on sunny days, because the steep valley sides create a shadow which quickly precludes spotting, especially if you are looking from the sunny side into the gloom. On such days an overall cloud cover is preferable in steep-sided valleys. The ideal is uniform high cloud, which often precedes a frontal system. Such conditions provide the ultimate sight fishing conditions in the steep valleys, but the direct opposite is true on wide, treeless plains, especially if there is also a strong wind.

Even a small trout can make a miserable wet, flooded day enjoyable. Zane Mirfin hoists a hard-earned prize aloft while Nigel Witting looks on. *Andrew Howe*

What to Look For

One of the most accomplished anglers we have guided is Jay Coulter from Bozeman, Montana. Jay is a serious, thinking angler who is a delight to guide because he places little emphasis on achieving success at every outing. Catching a few is a bonus. Blank days are accepted as part and parcel of the New Zealand experience. Everyone has them occasionally.

Graeme first guided Jay and his good friend, Todd Seymour, on the Wangapeka, a tributary of the Motueka which is among the most difficult of the local rivers for spotting fish in its middle and lower reaches. A brown algae forms on the rocks, which besides making the fish hard to see makes wading a perilous business. But despite rarely achieving more than modest success some local anglers like this area, preferring it in some ways to the heavily fished upper river, where the fish are easier to see.

This particular day was cloudless and the river was clearing rapidly after a sizable fresh. Great conditions, and the friends soon landed six or seven excellent fish, all of which Graeme spotted first. Jay was fascinated by the stalking, spotting method and insisted that Graeme explain all the cues he used to pick the fish up. None was easy to see, despite the near-perfect conditions, and those the men did see had to be pointed out to them first. Les Hill and Graeme tried to analyse these cues in *Stalking Trout*, and here they are briefly summarised as they are still relevant.

Brown trout are masters of camouflage.

A delicately spotted trout which had been living over sand and modified its colour accordingly.

Trout, especially browns, are masters of camouflage, adapting to the particular environment they find themselves in. Hence, resident fish in the fish-rich Arnold River flowing from Lake Brunner are often near-black on the back in keeping with the deeply stained water of the stream. By contrast the browns of the Styx, another Westland river, are handsome silver specimens more akin to sea fish than river dwellers. Not surprisingly the rocks of that stream are light-coloured schist. Yet despite this chameleon-like ability to disguise themselves the deception is never quite perfect. One of the first things to look for is a slightly discordant colour. If alerted first by a suspicious shape – the typical torpedo profile when viewed from above – then colour often confirms the diagnosis. In some back-country rivers healthy browns often display a handsome deep green colour – a dead giveaway to a skilled trout spotter.

Sometimes the clues are extremely subtle and may take the form of a flash of the white inside of the mouth as the fish engulfs a food item, or a momentary hint of a pale belly as it rolls to intercept some other morsel. Occasionally, the giveaway might simply be the tail movement over a light-coloured rock or even a lazily waving fin. Many a fish has betrayed its presence by the shadow cast on a light-coloured bottom of small, even-shaped material such as fine gravel or sand.

Above all, the initial suspicion is confirmed by movement. Unless a fish is almost comatose it will move some part of its body eventually. The highly obvious, dark-coloured fish found in calm, shallow water from time to time are not really worth bothering with. They are often spent fish, skinny and ugly in appearance and not long for this world. The serious angler is looking for the healthy, active specimens in the faster water.

Jay Coulter gave sight fishing his all and has become a very respectable spotter of fish. He admitted that the learning curve was steep, but through sheer concentration and determination he has gained confidence and proficiency. He often asked Graeme what it was that first alerted him to the presence of a fish. This was difficult to answer, as on some occasions it was a combination of factors all coming into play at the same time.

Often the very first fish of the day is the hardest to spot, possibly because the angle of light is not conducive to easy spotting early in the morning. Hence the reason why many New Zealand anglers are happy to hit the river at the 'crack' of 9.00am or later. But every situation is unique, and no two days on the same water are quite alike.

Ian Cole and Rob Bowler with a fish they had spotted and stalked in a Southland stream. *Jana Bowler*

Anglers can increase the odds by employing elementary techniques, which include treading quietly and avoiding the unnecessary movement of rocks. Most anglers stalk too quickly. High banks are great for spotting, but avoid showing your profile or the fish will be gone without your even knowing it was there. They don't give second chances. A spooked fish is a fish lost. All the same, careful use of the cover from an elevated position is the optimum spotting position, especially with two anglers working together. Of course it goes without saying that clothing that tones in well with the environment is essential.

Some experienced anglers are very adept at reading 'windows' in the current to spot fish feeding on the bottom in deep, fast water, arguably the most difficult place to find fish but also one of the most productive. From an elevated position it is possible at times to focus on a patch of calm surface water some metres upstream of the target area. By following the window downstream we have sometimes picked up fish that would normally be impossible to see. A heavily weighted nymph will sometimes fool these invariably big, strong specimens.

Sight fishing can be frustrating, and anglers sometimes despair of ever gaining a reasonable degree of proficiency. A large part of the whole business is linked to a combination of successful reading of the water and patience. When conditions are really difficult it is best to fish blind. While we would once have advocated persevering through thick and thin, experience tells us that blind fishing techniques can often be extremely successful. The key is being prepared to adapt.

BLIND FISHING

The term blind fishing is actually a misnomer as it suggests flogging the water in a haphazard and futile way. Nothing could be further from the

truth, as it is an extremely useful and versatile way to catch trout. While most streamer flies and downstream wetflies are fished blind, it is not necessarily chuck and chance. Dry fly and nymph are equally effective fished blind in the right circumstances.

Situations like this are prime blind fishing areas. Trout concentrate in the oxygen-rich shallows and are vulnerable to anglers' wares.

While much is written of the South Island's highly visible trout and sighted angling techniques, we have calculated that 60 per cent of our trout are caught by blind fishing. If we always waited for perfect conditions we would catch far fewer fish. We also realised a long time ago that, in many rivers, for every fish we could see there would be many more lying in very catchable positions. Blind fishing really involves exploring the water by casting flies into locations where you expect trout. After a while, water-reading skills become honed and you learn to trust your instincts as to trout location. When you start catching lots of fish you become a convert.

Blind fishing in the South Island is best exploited in conjunction with sight fishing techniques. Try to catch the fish you can see but also place a few well-directed casts into areas you cannot see into but suspect trout are present. Some rivers don't suit blind fishing because trout stocks are too low, but in rivers that have moderate to high fish populations it can be extremely effective.

Targeting the right locations is the major factor of success when blind

Another battle begins ... Note the tannin-coloured water which is characteristic of many West Coast streams. Trout can be tough to spot in such waters and blind fishing into strategic locations may well pay dividends.

fishing. We're often surprised at how many fish most people walk past. Sight fishing will often tell good anglers where the fish aren't lying, and a few well-placed casts into a suspected occupied lie will produce a hook-up.

Many anglers are so hung up on sight fishing that they run up the river, passing most of the catchable fish here. We now move more slowly and cover the water more thoroughly, depending on the weather, sighting conditions, fish populations and other factors. We've often followed other anglers through a piece of water that they have fished only hours earlier and caught more than they did. In many cases we suspect that those anglers actually herded the fish into places where they were more vulnerable to capture.

We are regarded as pretty decent fish spotters but we realise our limitations and have learned to trust our instincts as to where the catchable trout are. Believe us, we blind fish frequently.

CHAPTER 7

SOUTH ISLAND FLY-FISHING METHODS AND STRATEGIES

Much has been written about sight fishing in wilderness rivers, but the South Island trout fishery offers much more variety. It is a wise angler who is aware of all the options and periodically samples the different experiences available. Such knowlege and adaptability can enhance or even save many a fishing trip. To lock oneself into rigid patterns of fishing behaviour diminishes potential opportunities and certainly reduces the fun you can have learning and participating in great new angling activities.

DRY FLY FISHING

Watching a large brown trout lift off the streambed and softly ingest your high-floating dry fly has to be the ultimate South Island angling experience. Dry flies are great fun to fish and can be extremely effective. Recent advances in nymph fishing techniques have meant that many New Zealand anglers don't use dry flies as often as they should, but in the right conditions the dry fly is a lethal fish-catching tool producing large numbers of fish for the angler.

The dry fly is an effective catching tool because you can cover more water with a dry in a shorter time period allowing more efficient use of your time. Trout will generally come from further away to take a dry than a nymph, so it is effective in rivers with low densities of fish. Some rivers and lakes are better dry fly waters than others, although it can take a while to work this one out.

While probably 90 per cent of a trout's diet is made up of subsurface foods, trout are always on the lookout for surface foods. This is particularly so during the warmer months of the year when surface foods are more prolific, although fish will rise year-round if the food is available.

Weather conditions play a large part in the success of the dry fly. Hot, sunny, windy summer days are often ideal, but don't discount grey, cloudy,

A handsome trout taken on a Royal Wulff dry fly.

Wasp and cicada imitations: effective summer dry flies. *Martin Langlands*

drizzly days either. The real trick with fishing dries is to identify the dry fly potential of the day and to tie on the most effective imitation for the circumstances. South Island trout are opportunists and will eat a wide range of foods. Often the angler will observe a hatch and rising fish, but most fish caught on dries will be those cast at non-rising sighted fish or those fished blind.

Leaders for casting dries should be 3–5m (10–16 feet) long, depending on water conditions and timidity of trout. Tippets should be 1.5–4kg (3–8½lb) depending on fly size, the timidity of the trout, and water surface factors. Dry flies are a delight to cast and much easier than heaving weighted nymph rigs. Tailwinds on the water are preferable as they help to straighten the leader and assist presentation.

Placement of the dry can be critical to success. When casting to sighted fish that are close to the surface the dry can be dropped right in front of the fish and perhaps a little to one side. When fish are in shallow water they won't often see the fly unless it lands 10–20cm (4–8 inches) from their nose. Trout often respond best to a dry if they see it hit the water. Many anglers cast the fly too far ahead of the fish and by the time the fly reaches the fish it is dragging unnaturally.

Big flies often need to be placed further away as they hit the water harder and can startle wary fish. Nevertheless, large dries have their place in the

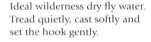

Ideal wilderness dry fly water. Tread quietly, cast softly and set the hook gently.

angler's arsenal as they will often pull fish up out of as much as 4 metres of fast-flowing water. We have seen many fish move 5–7m across clear pristine rivers to eat a big dry. Such flies can be deadly, fished blind through suspected lies at the right time of year.

The essence of South Island dry fly fishing. The trout is spotted, the cast is made and then suddenly there is that electrifying moment when hook and fish connect.

One great thing about dry flies is that it is really hard to miss a strike, unlike nymph fishing where trout often spit out the fly before you can strike. Most trout take the dry fly very deliberately and positively. Wait until the fish has the fly and has turned back under the water, then lift firmly to set the hook. Many anglers count '1, 2, 3 – strike'! Use whatever system suits you. Generally for smaller fish you should strike faster and for larger fish strike more slowly. Rainbows don't usually rise as freely to the dry fly as browns do, but when they do they generally take the fly faster.

If the fish follows the fly downstream and takes facing toward you, or you can see an eye as it faces sideways to you, then wait for it to turn upstream before you strike. A splashy rise often means a smaller fish, hence a faster strike. We prefer to be cautious on the dry fly strike. Often if you are too slow and you don't feel the fish, you may tie on a smaller fly and try again. Fast, premature dry fly strikes almost always see the fish dash for cover unhooked.

Dry flies are often viewed as slow-water flies. This is a mistake, as fish will take them in extremely fast water if they can see them. In summer when the fish are in more oxygenated waters they are particularly vulnerable to a well-placed dry. Don't ignore the universal rule of trout fishing: spend two-thirds of your time in the top one-third of the pool.

Learn to fish the dry fly with confidence. It's a great technique.

UPSTREAM NYMPH FISHING

It is said that nymphs comprise more than 90 per cent of a river trout's diet and that is why every serious South Island angler should learn to nymph fish effectively. If you have a nymph pattern drifting through the right areas at the right depth for enough time, success should be a certainty.

Upstream nymphing is relatively straightfoward, and it is a topic covered well in many American and some New Zealand books. Floating fly-lines and long tapered leaders are the basic equipment, and the fly is cast directly upstream or across and upstream and allowed to drift naturally.

Long leaders are essential for keeping the fly-line out of the trout's vision. This is especially important for blind fishing where you are not exactly sure of a potential victim's location. Long leaders offer enough nylon for the nymph to descend to the level of the fish. Fine tippets can be useful, as they offer less drag resistance and friction in the water and allow a nymph to sink faster and move more naturally.

Most anglers are not really successful with nymphs for two main reasons: the size of fly and the depth that the fly is presented. Fly size is related to food availability, water clarity, fish depth and fish preference. Generally larger nymphs work best in early season and in times of high water flow. Later in the season, when fish have seen anglers and water levels are dropping, smaller nymphs are more effective. Some rivers we know never fish well with large nymphs, and yet in other waterways the fish would almost crawl onto the bank to get a nice juicy #8 nymph. Headwater fisheries are often prime places for large nymphs, while more fertile lowland recreational fisheries are best fished with smaller nymphs.

The second main problem faced by nymph fishermen is getting the fly down to the fish. With increased angling pressure, fish are lying deeper, in faster water, and require a more precise imitation, which poses technical problems to the angler. Nymphs can be tied using heavy wire hooks, be weighted with lead and copper wire, or tied with beadheads (standard or tungsten) or beadchain eyes. Furs that absorb water, synthetic materials, and streamlined flies tied with plastic bodies are also useful. If that is not enough, products such as split shot, leadersink, lead-putty, etc, can help get the flies deeper.

Because fish are usually near the bottom in relatively heavy currents they tend to feed horizontally rather than vertically in the water column. Lifting off the bottom to take flies is not economic in food energy terms. Rainbows are often more willing to lift to take a fly even though they regularly reside in heavy feeding currents, whereas browns often require a presentation at their feeding level. Depth is often deceptive in flowing water, and many fish that appear to ignore a nymph pattern are probably not

Big fish, small fly. A good-sized brownie caught on a #24 Pheasant Tail nymph.

seeing the fly at the required depth within their feeding range. Fish can be selective too, so don't waste too much time on an unco-operative fish. Move upstream and locate a new target.

Line-mending skills are important in nymphing successfully and necessary to counteract drag from accelerating your fly and pulling it to the surface. Mending skills are especially important when you are nymphing cross-stream or in a combination of faster and slower water. Efficient fly-line manipulation can increase the amount of time your nymph stays in the strike zone and how natural it appears to the trout.

Casting nymph rigs can cause problems for many anglers. Heavy 'bombs', double nymph rigs and long leaders can cause serious cases of frustration. Remember to slow your casting stroke, open your casting loop, wait longer on the forward and backcasts to better load your rod; then casting those rigs won't be so bad. Consider using a heavier fly-line and rod for 'magnum' rigs.

A major problem with nymph fishing is strike detection. Experts in the US have said that anglers see only about 25 per cent of the takes that they get. We believe it. We see so many missed strikes, both on sighted fish and

A wilderness stream, an angler, a good cast … but is the nymph pattern a suitable size and weight for the conditions?

Various sized nymphs and typical strike indicators used for such flies.

Yarn strike indicators are prepared by forming a double slip knot in the leader at a suitable distance from the nymph, sliding in a suitable sized and coloured piece of yarn or wool then trimming to an appropriate size.

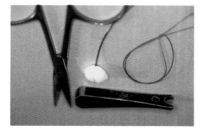

Construction of a yarn strike indicator: make a loop, slide through yarn, tighten loop and trim with snippers or scissors. Easy!

when blind fishing. Many of the problems come from not recognising a take. This can be remedied to some extent by a spotting partner on the bank communicating a take or through the use of strike indicators.

The biggest problem we see is that most anglers are too slow on the strike. Trout in our local area do not hold a subsurface fly in their mouths for very long. They can feel that the artificial nymph is a fake and will eject it immediately. As soon as the fish has the fly the angler should be vigorously setting the hook. Fast-action rods, non-stretch fly-lines and chemically sharpened hooks are very useful in this regard. However, the angler's reflexes are the most important factors. Nymph strikes should have the angler striking sideways with the tip of the rod while pulling on the fly-line with the other hand – assuming the angler already has good line control and there is direct contact between the angler and the fish. Often there is no more than a mini-second between a wasted opportunity and a solid hookup. Zane can remember taking Rob Bowler fishing on the Motupiko River and watching him miss several strikes in a row through striking too slowly. Rob wasn't used to fishing over such wary fish, which are often exposed to angling pressure. The Southland fish he was used to were much more obliging and would hold the nymph in their mouths a lot longer. When accused of having a 'Southland strike', he collapsed laughing.

As fish become more subject to angling pressure they will spit out the fly out a lot faster. Once you understand this and can counteract the technical problems of striking a fish taking your nymph, you will catch more.

Strike indicators

Usually nymphing rigs will be fished in conjunction with a strike indicator for detecting takes. Several non-indicator nymph fishing techniques work well for casting to sighted fish, but even for sighted fish, and especially blind fishing, a strike indicator helps. We use a number of different indicators, including foam, plastic, wool, synthetics, and acrylic glo-bug yarns. Strike indicators are often better than using a dry fly to indicate a take, because they are more visible and more aerodynamic, allowing anglers to fish nymphs in deeper, faster water. Strike indicators are also better performers in adverse weather and poor light conditions.

We find small yarn indicators the best all-round choice, either tied to the leader with a separate piece of nylon or with a simple overhand slip knot to hold them in place. Recently we have been using a double loop knot for indicators, which is easier to remove and doesn't kink or weaken the leader as much. Indicators should be small but dense, and trimming the top edge square every so often makes them float better and remain more visible. Liquid fly floatant dressings are best for waterproofing yarn indicators, as paste formulations often gum up the fibres and inhibit flotation.

Try to use natural colours such as off-white, green or yellow. Chartreuse greens and yellows are most visible and are our favourites. Brighter colours can spook wary brown trout, but rainbows will often happily go for them. Combination indicators using a 'fruit-salad' of colours can be useful in varying light conditions. Black is especially useful in extreme glare because it has a strong silhouette and can be seen when brighter colours are invisible or indistinguishable against the silvery glare of reflected light. We even have friends in Colorado who use small fluorescent light tubes as 'glow-in-the-dark' indicators.

A bushy dry fly being used as a strike indicator has a dropper attached to the bend of the hook.

Always try to use the smallest indicator practicable to avoid spooking fish. In our area we have developed some innovative techniques in the preparation and use of micro-indicators. Despite preferring to use small indicators, however, it is no good using an indicator that you cannot see, and we even use exaggeratedly large ones on occasion for anglers with poor eyesight and slow reflexes. They still catch fish, and most of the time the trout aren't too concerned, especially when fishing heavier water.

When blind fishing you should use an indicator that floats well and doesn't constantly sink, relaying false information of bogus takes. This can be extremely frustrating. Obviously drag-free presentations help indicator floatation and visibility. Fast-action rods can assist to dry indicators on occasional false casts through faster line speeds.

Some potential indicator materials: wool, synthetic yarn, plastic and foam stick-ons and coloured paste.

We have noticed that many anglers place their indicators too far from the fly. With increasingly alert fish, noticing a take and reacting before the fish can eject the nymph becomes more important. We've seen trout accept and reject nymphs before anglers can react when there is a gap of only 15–20cm (6–8 inches) between fly and indicator. Gaps between 30cm and 1.2 metres (that is, 1–4 feet) are standard for South Island nymphing rigs. Wary fish will often just bump the fly, resulting in the indicator giving a tiny shudder before continuing its drift uninterrupted. Be prepared to strike fast and at any signal. Often a pre-emptive strike is better than no strike at all, particularly on challenging fish. Remember you will usually get only one chance. Try hard to minimise wasted opportunities, but remember too that nobody is fast enough to hook them all.

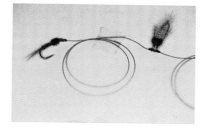

A tandem nymph rig illustrating how the dropper is attached via the eye of the top nymph.

Indicator nymphing rigs

Using a single nymph with an indicator is a very good technique when

Fishing with double rigs inevitably produces the occasional tangle.

angling to sighted fish or fishing larger stonefly or creeper imitations.

Double nymph rigs with an indicator are preferred blind fishing rigs. Two nymphs are often better than one because it can be easier to work out which nymph the trout like best on any particular day. It also gives the fish two choices, and allows you to fish at two different depths. You can use the same size nymphs or vary the sizes and patterns. We find that in summer, when trout get wary, two smaller weighted nymphs achieve the same depth but are preferred by trout to a single larger fly. Another trick is to use a large nymph as a sinker with a smaller more imitative nymph trailer, or alternatively use a beadhead or attractor nymph ahead of a more subdued standard nymph. The combinations are endless – it's entirely up to the angler's discretion and imagination.

Weighting the leader for nymph rigs

Sometimes the only way to get deep among the trout is to add additional weight to the leader. Split shot, lead strips and lead putty are all options here. Don't be afraid to slide a single brass or tungsten bead down the leader on top of a nymph tied without a beadhead to add additional weight and flash. Lead weights should be attached firmly above tippet knots or attached to droppers, etc., to avoid sliding around. Various amounts can be added to achieve the desired depth. Heavy rigs are terrible to cast but are often a necessary evil to access deep-lying fish unwilling to move upwards for a nymph. When casting remember to slow your stroke and open up your casting loop. When using a lot of lead use a more buoyant indicator such as foam or sticky-back indicators, and place them further from the fly to assist the sink rate. Such rigs are especially useful for catching rainbow trout in fast flows or brown trout in times of high, discoloured river flows.

SMALL WET FLY FISHING

Swinging a fly downstream is always fascinating, as it conjures up images of the ancient origins of our sport. The tap of a fish hitting the fly and a screaming reel with a self-hooked fish attached are classic experiences that have been largely replaced by visual observation of the strike and a manual hookset. It's kind of sad in a way, because wet fly fishing is so basic, yet so artful and relaxing. It helps to put the fun back into fly-fishing.

Fishing downstream with small wet flies has largely been superceded by modern dry fly and nymph fishing techniques because such methods are often more successful on South Island waters. Nevertheless, swinging a

pair of small wets across and downstream still has its uses and can produce fish when other methods are less viable. It is particularly successful
where there are moderate to high numbers of smaller fish.

Apart from the relaxing nature of this fishing method, it has the advantage of the fish hooking themselves. It is an ideal method for novices or
inexperienced casters to catch trout on a fly because the water pressure
straightens the line out. It is also useful when howling downstream gales
make standard upstream casts impossible.

The downstream wet fly is useful in low light conditions when visual
observation of a strike becomes difficult. Insects, particularly caddis, are
likely to be ascending to the surface and a wet fly presentation mimics this
activity. Fish do not mind movement in the flies and will often take as the
flies lift up through the water column. At the beginning or end of the day
trout will often be nearer the surface and may move further back in the
pools to tailout and calmer areas, where they become vulnerable to a well-
presented fly. Such fish are often feeding more avidly and are more
unsuspecting, and good numbers of fish can be caught.

The wet fly is also a very good daytime technique, particularly in shallow, stable, well-oxygenated ripples. This technique can be used to cover
quite large areas in a relatively short space of time, making it a good searching method. Small, soft hackled flies can be substituted with standard

Ideal downstream wet fly
water at the source of the
Buller, Lake Rotoiti.

weighted or beadhead nymphs for daytime use. This helps the angler to fish deeper in the water column. Reasonably heavy tippets should be used, as the weight of the fish and the current behind some takes can put a lot of pressure on the tippet. The rod should be held upright on about a 60-degree angle above the water to absorb the shock of the take. Most fish should hook themselves. Occasionally a small flick of the wrist may be required to set the hook, particularly in slower water or on longer casts.

Fish this method with confidence. It's great fun and effective too.

STREAMER FISHING

American Dave Goodhart and Zane stood on the bank, peering intently down through the native beech trees into the crystal-clear water. The pool was a classic – deep with plenty of structure – and the huge trout lying there was unmistakable. The only problem was that the fish was facing into a back eddy, vacuuming up all the easy pickings swirling around. Because the fish was facing downstream and the current was moving away from the angler, strike detection and drag were going to be major problems. Dave and Zane looked at each other, instantly aware of the inherent angling problems to be overcome. 'How about a streamer?' asked Dave.

A big black streamer fly imitating a small fish is very attractive to a brown trout.

A longish leader was connected, tapered to 2x with a huge black Woolly Bugger. To get the fly deeper we added a big AA split shot as well. It was time for action.

Dave climbed down into position and threw the streamer upstream, well beyond the fish's tail. He let it sink then started a fast retrieve, pumping the rod tip up and down. As the dark streamer passed the fish it snapped its head sideways to eyeball the intruder, then decided to attack. The fly was escaping fast and the fish accelerated across the small stream and hammered the streamer. The anglers could see every spot on the fish, its hooked, arrogant kype and its flashing white jaws. Dave's rod doubled over, and he let out a war whoop. The huge brown wallowed on the surface, then accelerated upstream through surging currents and boulders. After a great fight the big fish was landed and released, but the method used and the aggression of the take made it a great memory.

Angling with fish, crustacean, amphibian, and rodent imitations is often neglected in favour of more classic dry fly and nymph fishing methods. Yet many trout like to eat the 'big stuff', and in the right circumstances using it is extremely effective.

Streamers are usually fished under tension so the take is felt as an electrifying jolt, although they can be fished dead drift as well. Fast and slow retrieves coupled with deep or shallow streamers will produce in most rivers and stillwaters when used by the thrill-seeking angler. Evening and night fishing are often best, although daytime fishing can also work well. Coloured-water situations can be prime streamer times too. We've found autumn to be an excellent time for throwing a streamer, as browns are more aggressive before spawning and they often move into shallow ripply water where they are prime targets for a big, ugly streamer. Often such fish will be of above-average size and will hammer your fly with such aggression and anger that you won't believe it. Be careful, this sort of fishing can become addictive. We've spent hours flogging the water waiting for the next 'fix'.

MOUSE PLAGUES

From time to time, mouse numbers build up to levels that encourage heavy trout predation. Because mice are most active nocturnally, this is when the trout are most likely to eat them as they fall into rivers or consciously swim across 'lemming style'. Mouse mortality slows in dry warm years and mice numbers explode in years when native beech trees are seeding. Whatever the reason, trout love mice because they are a big bundle of food.

Rob Bowler with a 5.5kg (12lb) monster. When it was caught it was found to have two mice in its throat. *Pete Lapidus*

A diet of mice encourages prodigious growth in trout. Such fish have small heads and big bodies and are in superb condition. They commonly are 60–70cm long, weighing in at 4–5.5kg. Such a high-protein diet can make trout in any given river system 1–2kg heavier than normal and can produce numerous 4.5–6kg beauties. Often you can tell a mouse feeder when it regurgitates a half-eaten mouse, or you can feel the hard furry nuggets in its stomach as you release it. Be especially careful when handling and releasing such obese fish, as it is far easier to damage them than more streamlined standard trout.

Despite the fact that most mice are eaten nocturnally, these fish are still accessible to nymph and dry fly anglers during the day by normal means. However, night fishing can be a good way to catch outsize fish, especially if they have been sighted in promising pools during the day but have been uncatchable.

Skating deerhair mice imitations and/or big steelhead dries can be deadly. There is no doubt as to when a fish has taken your imitation; these surface takes can be heart-stopping. Use heavy line and hold on tight. They always seem much larger in the dark.

Mice aren't the only large creatures that trout eat. Frogs and rats are also eaten. Zane had one lady angler who hired one of his spinning rods at

Too slow! A mouse and possible imitations.

Lake Rotoiti and managed to catch a nice fish for her dinner. She found a full-grown chaffinch in its stomach. Now, there's a challenge for some innovative fly tyer.

SEASONAL ASPECTS OF TROUT LOCATION AND MOVEMENT

Trout move around constantly. Often an individual fish may stay in the same area all year, but new fish will constantly move through this water both upstream and down.

Sometimes it is hard to work out if fish are sea-runs, have been there all along, or have just migrated from some other part of the river. As anglers we all have our own theories but our guess is that a little bit of everything is true. Anyway, what's important is that the fish are present and catchable.

Fish movements are generally in response to some environmental or biological stimulus. Water volume, temperature, time of year, food sources and spawning activity are obviously important. The following comments are some basic observations we have made over the years.

Many small streams, (both rainbow and brown fisheries) fish well prior to Christmas before river levels drop and temperatures rise, forcing fish to drop back into larger water systems. Most of these fish move into streams to spawn during autumn and winter and over-winter if conditions are favourable. Such small stream fish are often larger than average.

Many larger, braided, alluvial rivers fish best in mid- to late season as water levels drop and water clarity becomes more favourable for sight fishing. Reduced water flows mean that locating fish and their preferred habitat is simplified, leading to increased catch rates. Such rivers maintain cool water temperatures year-round, making them prime areas in times of drought. Before Christmas such rivers are generally unfishable, as spring snow-melt usually means high, discoloured water flows for the first few months of the fishing season.

Many rivers feeding into high-country lakes fish better after Christmas as trout migrate upstream to take advantage of seasonal food sources. Sea-run fish in estuaries are generally more plentiful in spring and summer.

Some headwater reaches of rivers fish best in autumn as schools of smaller fish migrate upstream to spawn and repopulate upper stretches.

Larger freestone rivers often offer the most consistent fishing during low-water/high-temperature periods. As water temperatures soar, fish will increasingly move into mid-river, fast water and other highly oxygenated areas. Brown trout will often congregate in the extreme heads of fast shallow runs, making them easy targets for nymph and indicator fishing. In

Small streams can provide some interesting flyfishing experiences, particularly in early season or in times of higher flows.

Milky alluvial water early in the season makes for nice photos but tough fish spotting.

such conditions 80 per cent of the trout population may be living and feeding in 20 per cent of the river. Fish will often congregate where cooler tributaries enter or anywhere springs and cool upwellings may lower the water temperature a few degrees.

There are all sorts of scenarios here, often with no apparent rhyme or reason to them. Many anglers bemoan the fact that some streams are ruined or thrashed, but usually it is because they do not understand the subtle nuances of the factors that constitute a fishery. It takes time and effort to attempt to understand these factors, and the more time you spend fishing the more likely you are to encounter these situations and, more importantly, be in a position to predict their occurrence. Every river system has an individual pattern of fish behaviour. Fishing the same waterways at varying locations and times of year will give you more insight into fish behaviour which should translate into more fish caught.

WINTER FISHING

In most regions in the South Island the fishing season traditionally closes at the end of April each year. This allows predominantly brown trout fisheries to be unmolested by anglers when spawning begins in early winter. Besides, after a seven-month trout season many of us have had enough of fishing and are starting to show more interest in the local duck population. However, there are plenty of opportunities for fishing in the winter for those die-hard fishing fanatics who can't help themselves.

Winter can strike at any time! Scott and Stuart Mirfin brave out an unseasonal squall at Lake Tennyson.

The fishing regulations vary between Fish and Game regions, and a quick read of the South Island fishing regulations will soon tell you where you can go and what you can do. Most of the best locations will usually be closed for the winter, but more prime areas are being opened up during winter as the minimal impact of winter angling is being realised and there is increased demand for it by licence holders. Winter fishing areas are often popular recreational fisheries, with high trout populations in the lower reaches and estuaries of rivers that are not heavily fished during the summer. Headwater reaches are normally closed for spawning and rest purposes.

Some of the best winter fishing in May is in the Southern Lakes and Fiordland regions, where many predominantly rainbow fisheries are open until the end of May. Although it can get a bit cold, the rainbows are feeding vigorously, and even some good dry fly fishing can occur. Some anglers of our acquaintance rave about it.

During May through early July, most browns are in spawning mode and many will be away spawning in small tributary streams. The fish that remain in more exposed waters open to fishing will often be less intent on feeding and more concerned with chasing each other. Such spawning fish are often more aggressive and will still eat nymphs and egg flies. Streamers can work well, although don't discount dry fly action. Remember, too, that not every fish in the river will be thinking about spawning and many beautifully conditioned maiden fish should be available to catch. Nelson locals swear that May is one of the best dry fly months on the lower Motueka River on sunny days. We have caught cruising browns on dry flies in Lake Rotoiti during August, so there are no hard and fast rules.

Browns are often in poor condition in winter because of spawning but by late spring have regained condition. Rainbows generally spawn in the July-to-September period and are in their poorest condition in spring. As a result many high-country and rainbow fisheries in the South Island open as late as November to allow fish longer to recover condition.

With winter fishing, air temperature and weather usually dictate fishing success and enjoyment. It is best to fish on calm, sunny days, after the chill of morning frost is waning. Because of the short winter days and fewer sunshine hours, 10.00am till about 3.00pm usually provides the best of the fishing, especially if you are trying to sight the occasional fish. Late in the afternoon, the water turns black because of the low sun angle. This makes it nearly impossible to spot fish, see your strike indicator, or identify productive trout lies.

Trout can be anywhere, with browns typically in shallower and calmer water and rainbows preferring deeper, faster water. Exceptions do occur, so it pays to work out such factors on a day-by-day basis. In winter you should use brighter coloured flies, including attractor patterns, and fish deeper because fish are usually less active and won't move as far to take the fly.

The great thing about fishing at this time of year is the crisp fresh air, impressive winter scenery, and virtually no other anglers. We know of many anglers who prefer this time of year for these reasons.

FISHING IN ADVERSE WEATHER CONDITIONS

Despite the stories you hear, the books and magazines you read, and the angling photographs you're shown, the South Island gets its share of horrific weather. Most videos and photos you may see (including those in this book) are only filtered slices of reality. When you go fishing here you should always take rain gear, and waders are always an excellent choice if you suspect bad weather. Your first priority should be to stay dry and warm, then despite the environmental conditions it is usually possible to catch at least some fish.

Many days of angling will include cold, wet, windy, unpleasant conditions that are bearable with the right equipment. South Island rivers often take incredible amounts of rain to make them rise, and on days like these the fishing may be remarkably good. Some rivers fish well as they are ris-

Campbell Whyte with a Lake Mapourika brown on a grey day.

Crossing a swift-flowing river safely. *Leif Milling*

Spring creeks offer angling opportunities after bad weather. Here a late season front has deposited rain and snow which have discoloured the main river.

ing, but the best time is when the river is falling after a fresh. This is where previous experience is useful – to know which rivers or lakes are most likely to be fishable after heavy rainfall. Headwater regions are usually the first to clear, but often such areas are not an option due to the difficult access and time constraints. Fortunately, the South Island has such a large number of rivers and water catchments within a relatively short geographical distance, that a drive into another catchment will often find fishable water.

Sometimes a whole region will be affected, and anglers wanting to fish will have to be adaptable. Fish can be caught in amazingly discoloured water; the trick is to find somewhere that fish are concentrated and where you are able to make a decent presentation without drowning. Treat New Zealand rivers with respect; they have brought about the demise of a few careless anglers. If a river is visibly rising, get to safety immediately. Many times we've been stuck in places we shouldn't have been. If in doubt, don't do it.

Despite all of the above, knowledgable anglers should be able to take fish on all but the most abysmal days. Spring creeks, flooded lake edges, clear stream confluences, and lake inlets, all offer hope for the determined angler. High, discoloured water can actually be turned to advantage, as big trout are often most vulnerable at this time. Because they need to feed almost constantly, they often come close to shore to escape the current and to feed in the clearer edge locations. Edges, grass banks, side channels,

and rocky structure are likely places to investigate. As the fish could be anywhere it is best to concentrate on the most obvious places and pools.

Upstream nymphing is the best way to catch such fish. Use stout leaders and strike indicators to fish large, brightly coloured nymphs. A little thought, innovation and persistence has put some big fish in the net for us when nobody thought it was possible. Although no one would choose to fish in such conditions it will definitely make you a better angler.

Hook-up on a dreary West Coast day.

EVENING FISHING

Classic sight-fishing is the predominant angling method of many New Zealand anglers, but fishing the evening rise has its charm too. Evening is a wonderful time to fish, especially in the summer. Many anglers, after having fished all day, miss the best action. Fish metabolism often increases as insect activity begins and water temperatures drop. Standing in the dulling light with mountains outlined against blood-red skies, surrounded by swarms of hatching bugs and porpoising fish, is an angler's dream. It's rare to ever see another angler – most have gone home hours earlier.

Best results are to be had on warm, calm, settled evenings when insect hatches are most likely. Staking out a likely pool, run or lake bank and waiting for the fish to announce their presence is a good technique . Try to position yourself so you can see the water against the last of the evening light. Fishing surface flies to rising fish is fascinating but can prove frustrating if they are selective. Luckily most of the time fish will be fairly obliging and that's why evening fishing is ideal for novice or less skilled anglers. A good ploy in very dull light, where the fish are consistently rising but the fly cannot be seen is to cast to the rises or splashes in the dark, count to three or five, then cast again. Often fish will be hooked when you lift off for another cast.

Trout can be feeding on midges, caddis, terrestrials, spent spinners, emergers, etc., so common sense usually dictates your choice of fly. Don't neglect downstream wet flies and streamers. Keep an open mind and be adaptable. Sometimes fish that are virtually impossible to catch in heavily fished streams become vulnerable in the evening.

NIGHT FISHING

Fishing in the pitch black of darkness is a frightening concept for many, but the technique is undoubtedly effective. There is method to the madness. Brown trout, in particular, are creatures of the night and will often come close to shore in search of forage fish.

Evening solitude in the search for rising trout.

Night fishing is distinct from evening fishing, in that you usually cannot see anything, and everything is done by feel. Moonlit nights are generally a waste of time. Obviously, you should always make sure you have a good torch or flashlight with you, as well as spare batteries and bulb.

Careful choice of water is the most important factor in being successful. Choose locations that encourage a density of fish, such as large pools, deltas, lake outlets, springs, and estuary points. Most people fish the wrong locations. If you couldn't catch fish in a whitewater torrent during the day, you can't expect to catch them there at night either. The most efficient way to be in the right place is to have checked it out before dark. Avoid wading in fast, deep water or areas laden with soft mud, snags or logs. Try to fish off the river bank. Lakes, particularly at the confluence of inflowing and outflowing streams, are often prime places to catch above average trout and generally offer safer footing than in a river. Canterbury's Lake Ellesmere, particularly at the mouth of the Selwyn River, routinely produces brown trout in the 5-10kg range for those hardy souls prepared to brave the darkness, the mud and the eels …

Most night fishing will be done with streamers or surface lures representing small fish, crustaceans or rodents. Such fishing is equally effective in rivers, stillwaters and estuaries. Floating lines are most often used as they are the easiest to control when there is no vision and everything must be done by feel and experience. The best technique is usually a slow retrieve, creeping your streamer along near the bottom, hoping to intercept a hungry trout. Takes can be subtle, so strike with a sideways movement of the rod. More often than not, however, a strong hit, surface boil, and adrenaline rush indicate a solid hook-up.

Dry flies can be fished dead drift and the angler can wait for the sound of the take. The best method though, is to move the fly in order to feel the take. Skating flies, such as a big Goddard caddis or steelhead waker flies, can be a good technique. Use mega-heavy tippet and hold on tight.

Summer is the most pleasant time for night fishing – it's warmer, although you have to wait longer for it to get dark. Rivers that often seem dead by day come to life after dark. Fish good locations and you will be consistently successful, particularly on brown trout. It is amazing what you can pull out of waters that are thrashed during daylight hours. Best of all, you will probably have them all to yourself.

ESTUARY FISHING

The great things about estuary areas are the birdlife, the smell of the sea

Some favourite night-time baitfish imitations. Clockwise from top left: Mrs Simpson, Craig's Night-time, Scotch Poacher, Black Woolly Bugger, Brown Beadhead Bugger.

and the miracle of tides. There is always something going on, and even if the fishing isn't great there are always things to look at. The fact that estuarine areas are among the most productive habitats on earth makes them not a bad place to fish either. Estuarine areas are defined as locations under tidal influence. Most rivers that drain into the sea in the South Island will have trout present at least some time during the year.

Tides have a large influence on such fisheries and the food chain. Brown trout will sometimes move into the lower stretches of rivers on the incoming tide and retreat on the falling tide. Most trout will hold in the river, however, and allow the tide to come and go, making good targets in holding pools at low tide. These factors are very dependent on the situation and circumstances, and anglers should approach the water with an open mind. Rainbows aren't well known for their sea-run behaviour in New Zealand, although it is possible to catch smaller school rainbows in estuarine tidal-influenced stretches of the Pelorus River in Marlborough.

The best time to fish estuarine areas is in spring and summer, when the trout congregate to take advantage of seasonal food sources such as bullies, smelt, whitebait, crabs, shrimps and small flounders.

A small estuarine brown which has taken a purple Flash-a-Bugger at the Wairau Bar.

Most success will be had using streamer-type flies imitating small fish. After dark is a particularly good time to catch trout in such areas, but you need to know the area and be extremely careful, especially on a rising tide. Daylight is still a good time to fish, but fly retrieves should be faster and the food imitations smaller.

Often there can be a conflict in spring with whitebaiters who line riverbanks near the tidal zone in pursuit of that elusive delicacy. A boat is handy for access up and down river, allowing you to reach to unwadeable areas and good structure, avoiding other recreational users, and making fishing time more enjoyable and productive.

The South Island has thousands of coastal trout waters that are largely unfished and populated by 2–3kg trout that are strong, silvery, thickly muscled, orange-fleshed specimens. To locate feeding fish, look for silver flashes, bow waves and small fish scattering, or just fish blind.

Trout are best caught over river gravel bottoms when fly-fishing. Mudflat areas mostly produce kahawai and flounder. Larger bodies of water are best covered by trolling or harling to cover as much territory as possible. (Duckshooting companions on the Riverton Estuary, which drains the Aparima River in Southland, told of the excellent trout fishing they have there, trolling silver toby lures behind an aluminium dinghy.)

CHAPTER 8

LAKE AND STILLWATER FISHING

Stillwater fishing has to be one of the South Island's best-kept secrets. Most anglers are oblivious to the quality of angling available.

The South Island has such an abundance of good trout water that stillwaters and lakes have often not received the recognition they deserve. Most anglers rush to the well-known streams, leaving the lake edges abandoned and opening up myriad opportunities for anglers who are prepared to explore the stillwater challenge.

South Island stillwaters often have excellent water clarity, offering superior sight-fishing opportunities to cruising fish. Stillwater guru Ian Cole of Wanaka is convinced that New Zealand has the best stillwater sight fishing in the world. Ian feels that a lack of knowledge of lake fisheries by anglers is why they are so often neglected.

Small inland lakes offer some special experiences.

Success in picking up a trout fossicking for food in a grassy channel.

The South Island has a vast range of stillwaters mostly formed through glaciation, flooding and hydro-electricity generation. They can also include tarns, backwaters and lagoons. They range in colour and clarity from blue to green to brown and every shade in between. They can be crystal clear like the Fiordland lakes, opaque milky blue like the Waitaki hydro lakes, or the tannin brown of the South Westland stillwaters. Every lake requires a slightly different approach, but this is the lure of stillwater angling.

Some lakes in the South Island rival rivers in terms of fish production, although the majority are poor in nutrients and fertility. Most of these waters are fairly acidic and have poor productivity compared with the many highly alkaline lakes in North America, which produce phenomenal numbers of fish. There are exceptions to this rule in New Zealand, the most notable being the volcanically formed 'fish factory' of Lake Taupo and other North Island lakes such as Rotorua, Tarawera and Aniwhenua, which support world-class rainbow fisheries. These lakes are tremendously fertile and support many mainstay food sources such as smelt and koura, which assist trout production. Most South Island lakes lack such high productivity, although notable exceptions do exist. North Canterbury's Lake Ellesmere, a huge coastal lagoon, has vast food supplies of silveries and bullies, and regularly produces trout up to 10kg. Some localised reservoirs and ponds in Otago likewise can produce outstanding fish densities and sizes.

Brown trout are the major catch of the South Island stillwater angler, because these less fertile, more acid waters best suit browns. They are more prone to cruise and feed close to shore in shallow water, where they are vulnerable to the well-prepared angler and where they offer the best sight fishing opportunities. Such brownies are cunning and can be difficult to

Lake Emily, home of brook trout.

deceive, but they are even more devious once hooked – diving around hidden snags or into dense weedbeds.

Rainbow trout are available in many lakes throughout the South Island. They are most prevalent in some Canterbury lakes, Waitaki hydro lakes, and Southern and Fiordland lake systems. Rainbows typically occupy territories different from those of brown trout in lakes; they are not as free-rising and are best caught on subsurface fly imitations. They usually do not patrol the shallow lake margins and are most often caught along deeper drop-offs and land features that are closer to deeper, more open water. Most rainbows are taken blind fishing with floating and sinking lines, as it is often difficult to sight fish effectively for them. They often take savagely and fight explosively on the surface, with sizzling runs that really get the adrenaline pumping.

Other fish species available to the South Island stillwater angler are several species of landlocked salmon, namely chinook, sockeye, and even

Atlantics, as well as brook char and mackinaw. Unfortunately cutthroat and golden trout were never released into New Zealand alpine lakes. Some Canterbury lakes also hold stocks of splake, a cross between brook char and mackinaw.

Both brookies and mackinaw are members of the char family, and unfortunately only limited angling opportunities exist here. Brook char can be caught in Lake Emily, where they commonly attain weights of 1–2.5kg, and are usually caught near the bottom with nymph and bully imitations. Mackinaw are present only in Lake Pearson and prefer deep cold water. Lake Pearson is currently open for fishing in very early spring as part of the winter fishing season.

WHERE THE FISH LIVE AND FEED

In stillwaters there are specific areas where the fish will congregate. If you are in the right place you can just wait for the fish to come to you, rather than having to move large distances to locate them (as you may do in a river fishery). Where rivers flow in and out of lakes are very likely areas. Often the first few hundred metres of lake outlets are especially fertile and support large caddis populations. In inlet areas food is constantly washed into lakes, attracting trout on a regular basis. Other places to look include shallow areas out to about 5m (16 feet), which are the most fertile and productive areas of stillwaters, as well as drop-offs and weedbeds.

Seasonal factors such as water level, temperature, time of day, wind direction and velocity, angling pressure and food sources all play a part in fish behaviour and their catchability. Trout in stillwaters are often 'moody'

Hook-up at Lake Benmore: Alan Campbell is optimistic about the size of the prize.

The Ahuriri arm of Lake Benmore offers some excellent stalking water.

and may not feed all day. Just because you are not seeing or catching fish does not mean they are not present.

Alan Campbell, of Omarama, and Zane were fishing the Ahuriri arm of Lake Benmore late in May 1997. Conditions were perfect – a lovely sunny morning, classic sandflats and weedbeds in shallow water. After several hours not a single fish had been seen, but Alan assured Zane that there were normally plenty of targets available. They finally came to the conclusion that most of the brown trout must have been up the river spawning, but as time progressed into the early afternoon a few fish appeared along the drop-offs, and some good directions from Alan, who was up on a high bank, soon had Zane hooked into a nice brownie. It became apparent that those fish not spawning upriver had retreated into deeper water at the onset of winter and only after the sun had warmed the water did they move into shallower water.

WHAT LAKE FISH EAT

Stillwater trout behaviour generally depends on what food sources are doing at the time, so a knowledge of insect and forage fish behaviour should help to improve your catch rate.

Midges are the most common year-round food source in lakes, but larger food sources are more easily imitated and offer a larger meal for hungry trout. Mayflies and caddisflies are common around inlet and outlet areas, but usually damselfly and dragonfly nymphs are more important in lakes, especially around weedbeds. Forage fish such as bullies, silveries and small eels are all important, as are crustacea such as koura.

Terrestrials are very important during the summer. Beetles in all shapes and colours, blowflies, wetas and cicadas are all of local and seasonal significance. Snails and waterboatmen can also be significant food sources.

We've always caught our largest lake fish with streamer patterns after dark. Large dark patterns, which give a good silhouette underwater, can provoke a vicious response.

The diet of a stillwater trout: adult dragonflies and damselfly nymphs are common fare.

HOW TO CATCH STILLWATER TROUT

The most important rule with stillwater angling is to look and think before you cast. There is no need to rush into the water; often it is best to fish from the bank, stay away from the water's edge, and keep a low profile.

The name 'stillwaters' implies that there is usually little water movement, so the lake angler will often have to move the fly to attract a response and use a relatively tight line so he can feel a take.

Typical stillwater nymphs and streamers.

Sight fishing is effective, and casting to a sighted feeding trout is very exciting. But such fish are often quite cunning. Flies can be cast straight at fish and will be taken on occasion, but leading the fish by 3–10m (10–30 feet), and allowing the trout to cruise onto the imitation, can also be very effective. The best method is to study the feeding beat of a fish and cast the fly into the anticipated feeding zone. The next time the fish cruises near the imitation, twitch it up off the bottom. If the fish shows interest and opens its mouth, then you should slowly but firmly tighten up and see if

Prime stillwater nymphs (clockwise from top left): dragonfly, snail, midge, damselfly.

An open area among vegetation at Lake Poerua, a likely location for cruising brownies.

Trout often cruise close to the bank on weedy overgrown shores.

the fish has taken it. If you are fishing a dry fly the take will be obvious.

Try swimming sub-surface imitations on a tight line so that you can feel the take – then there is no doubt when the fish has the fly. Anglers should point their rod tip directly at the fly or even have it under the water surface so there is direct contact and no slack between the fly and the angler. Sub-surface stillwater takes can be aggressive or subtle, and anglers should be firm but gentle on the hookset, as fish will often break off if held too tight. Because there is no downstream current and the fish are generally facing towards the angler, it is easy to break off large and even smaller fish on the hookset, especially when they shake their head or wallow on the surface.

Blind fishing is very effective in lakes once you have isolated fish territories and possible food imitations. Dry fly, nymphs and streamers all work well fished blind. Floating lines work, although they can leave a surface wake, and therefore long, finely tapered leaders are best. Sub-surface intermediate lines can be deadly. The new clear-coloured intermediate lines that sit just under the surface are excellent; they cast little shadow, create no ripple, are not affected by wind on the surface and communicate a take to the angler immediately. Sinktip and full sinking lines are very handy for getting deep with big nymphs and streamers. Sinking lines are great for catching rainbows, useful for drifting along behind a boat, and the heavier lines such as the Teeny 300-500 are excellent for harling streamers behind an electric motor.

Developing stillwater fishing skills can take some time, but it is worth the effort. The lakes and stillwaters of the South Island can offer some exhilarating, exciting and largely unexplored angling opportunities.

A perfect day on Lake Wakatipu.
Jana Bowler

GETTING TO THE WATER

New Zealanders have guarded the rights of access to waterways and mountains so much, that very large stretches of coastline, rivers and the shores of lakes have automatic right of access along them under 'The Queen's Chain', enshrined in law in the days of Queen Victoria, and designed to negate the problems so evident in modern-day Britain, where virtually all the best fishing and shooting is controlled by wealthy private interests. To some degree the Queen's Chain works here to this day, but there are anomalies and some quite significant problems. The first is that for various reasons many kilometres of waterway remain under riparian ownership, which effectively means that the landowner whose land adjoins the stream, lake or in a few instances, coastline, has the right to deny access along the shore, and this actually extends to the middle of the stream in the case of rivers. In reality very few landowners in the South Island apply their riparian rights to the letter of the law. Access up and down rivers and streams is largely unimpeded if that access has been gained legally – from some public access point, for example. Yet, at times we have been ordered off stretches of water in the Nelson district and other parts of the South Island by the landowner; we had no idea that we were trespassing and found the experience infuriating and humiliating. Thus it can be seen that public right of access cannot be taken for granted beyond a certain point, even if the local Fish and Game Council has erected fishing access signs.

The real threat to public access to many prime fisheries is simply a locked gate and/or an intimidating sign indicating that no access to that fishery is available across the adjoining land. Farmers, foresters and lodge owners all have their reasons for excluding access to all but their friends and paying visitors. Such situations are commonplace now, and with farmers in this country facing hard times the temptation to restrict access in return for cash is easy to understand. Like it or not, attitudes are changing rapidly, and we shall see more and more restriction of public access to public lands

Absolutely no access. Murchison farmer Wal Thorneycroft demonstrates a slight impediment to getting home after a day of fishing on his farm.

Swing bridges are often your access points to the back country. *Rob Bowler*

by those with self-interest at heart. Sometimes the problem of access is related to the carving up of larger blocks of land into so-called 'lifestyle' blocks, meaning that even a well-intentioned angler who seeks and obtains the right of access to a stream from one landowner may suddenly find he has strayed onto the property of a less-generous neighbour without knowing it. We have experienced this scenario and the embarrassment it causes.

It is not all doom and gloom. The majority of landowners are happy to allow access across their land to fishing areas. In most instances a courteous request for access will be met with a positive response. Most New Zealand farmers are genuinely interested in people and will stop to chat if they are not in the middle of a task. Reading the situation is important. If the farmer is in the middle of shearing, drenching or haymaking it is probably not wise to take up too much of his or her time.

It is essential that other protocols are observed. Always leave gates as they are found. Drive with consideration through livestock, especially when new lambs are about, and don't trample crops. In short, apply common sense to the situation. If a farm animal appears to be in trouble, assist if you can but also report the incident. Such actions will ensure mutual goodwill. Some farmers don't fish themselves but appreciate the taste of trout. It is often politic to ask if they would like one brought back, should you have a successful day.

Much public land with excellent access is still available on the conservation estate, but at the time of writing the Department of Conservation (DOC) is beginning to insist that professional guides hold concessions or permits. While some guides already hold these concessions the Professional Fishing Guides Association is working towards an agreement with DOC that will give members of the association automatic concession rights.

Follow instructions and you will ensure fishing access for generations to come.

HELICOPTERS

More and more is being written about the adventure and benefits of accessing wilderness areas by helicopter, and many local and overseas anglers are using choppers to transport them to fantasyland. We've had some awesome fishing trips using them to take us into the back country: they can save a lot of time and avoid the need to hump heavy gear across miles of rugged and inhospitable bush country.

But the truth is that most of the best fishing water in the South Island doesn't require a helicopter for access. Most wilderness rivers and headwater reaches can be reached within a hard day of walking from the closest road, so there are plenty of opportunities for anglers who are prepared to walk.

Many anglers also make the mistake of thinking wilderness trout will be stupid and that they will catch large numbers. This can happen, but anglers should visit such places for the experience rather than a trout body count. It is illogical to calculate trout caught into dollar terms spent on chopper transport. The two factors are entirely separate. Have realistic expectations and you will have an enjoyable wilderness helicopter trip.

Helicopters are great machines and do save a lot of time and effort. However, there are a number of factors to consider. You should fly only with reputable operators who are fully trained and have extensive experience. Good-quality, fully serviced and well-maintained machines are not inexpensive to hire, but give good peace of mind. There are a few rough operators out there who are driving some flying rust-buckets. Don't travel in flying lawnmowers that offer cheap rates, as such services do not include funeral costs.

'Have we made the right decision?' The helicopter departs, and we're on our own. *Georges Lenzi*

Never talk a pilot into flying if the weather isn't good. We've had excited customers con pilots into flying in highly marginal, abysmal conditions. Such flights are not fun, and our advice in such conditions is simple: Don't do it. There is plenty of other good water out there that you can drive to.

Always arrange a pick-up time and a contingency plan in case the weather deteriorates or something else happens. Make sure you memorise landing locations and other geographical features. Remember that everything looks totally different from ground level.

Always walk toward or away from the *front* of a landed helicopter, even when the blades are not revolving. Make sure you are within sight of the pilot at all times, and always follow his commands. Never walk around the side or back of a chopper because the pilot can't see you and the tail rotor

Helicopters: great for getting quickly into the back country, and especially useful for checking out the presence of other anglers.

Untracked wilderness becomes accessible by helicopter.

could really ruin your day. Always stoop down when approaching and leaving the front of the chopper, as certain difficult landing sites may mean the main rotor blades are not as high as you may think.

Always carry rods parallel to the ground to avoid poking them into the helicopter blades. Do not throw equipment out of or near the chopper, as it may get sucked into the rotors. And don't wave to your friends as you climb aboard. One Japanese tourist did and lost his hand.

Anglers should be ready for the chopper well before the appointed pick-up time. Find a suitable open landing site and make it easy for the pilot to land. Different makes and models of helicopter can tolerate different levels of landing sites. Hughes 500 D and E models are more manoeuvrable, having more ground clearance and better landing skids for rough terrain than, say, a Squirrel. Make it easy for the pilot to locate you by waiting in the middle of the riverbed, waving your arms, wearing an item of bright clothing, or preferably doing all three.

When first flying into an area, you should make a point of getting the pilot to buzz the area you intend to fish, to check for anglers already present. A skilled pilot should be able to check out a riverbed with enough height to avoid spooking fish and keep the helicopter's shadow off the water. Look hard for other anglers and if others are already there go somewhere else well out of their way. Before you set off on any chopper trip you should have a contingency plan for a few other locations in case somebody has beaten you to your first choice.

Anglers who are already fishing in a river have a responsibility to heli-copter-borne anglers to make themselves visible if they hear a chopper coming. We've experienced some nightmare scenarios where anglers al-

Will we see the chopper later in the day? Safety equipment, including personal locator beacons, is an advisable precaution in the back country. People can – and do – get lost.

ready in the river have hidden at the sound of the chopper and reappeared once the chopper has deposited its cargo and departed. These foolish people then either threatened and berated the new arrivals, or turned everybody's day into a marathon race upriver. Believe us, you do not want to land if there's going to be conflict with other anglers.

If a chopper is flying upstream and you are already in the river, odds are that they will have left you a day or two of fishing water. Most reputable helicopter operators are concerned to protect their reputation and will not knowingly 'jump' you. You should keep fishing upstream from your current position rather than race upstream for hours in a futile attempt to get ahead of the new arrivals. Remember even in wilderness rivers that possession is nine-tenths of the law. If you are camping make sure you are on the water before 9.00 am to avoid unpleasant surprises.

Homeward bound! Be careful entering and exiting helicopters.

People talk of wilderness areas being ruined by chopper pressure or thrashed to death, but the reality is that such angling pressure is there for only two months in mid-summer – and this is very dependent on weather conditions. Many wilderness areas can be inaccessible for weeks on end because of adverse weather.

Those who have tried it agree that the helicopter wilderness experience is well worth the cost and allows anglers with limited time or physical limitations to enjoy the wilderness.

FOUR-WHEEL-DRIVE VEHICLES

With the easing of import restrictions on Japanese-made vehicles, many New Zealanders now own some form of 4WD vehicle. They are great for reaching splendid off-road locations, but be sure you have permission to cross private land. Be especially sensitive to farmers' concerns during lambing and mustering times, or during daily dairy-milking activities. Always leave gates as you found them.

Anglers should always carry basic safety equipment with them. Tools such as a fold-up shovel, tow rope, hand-winch, anchor for no-tree situations, battery jumper leads, tyre-weld, and so on, have got us out of some tricky situations.

A uni-mog: the ultimate in overland transport for access to those really remote and difficult locations.

Be careful driving and turning around. We have sometimes found outselves in embarrassing situations when we have had to ask farmers to haul the vehicle out of places we should not have got into in the first place, and we have had to assist plenty of other poor souls as well. If a farmer or someone else has to haul you and your mates out of a ditch, then a couple of dozen beers as a thank-you gift is an appreciated goodwill gesture.

The trick to safe off-road driving is to have a well-maintained vehicle and learn to drive cautiously, anticipating potential problems before they occur. Most fishing locations can be accessed by the family car and then walking another 200 metres. We've found that it's the last 10 metres that usually causes problems!

A 4WD and a jetboat: the perfect combination for getting to the larger eastern alluvial waterways and their tributaries.

JETBOATS

Jetboats are fantastic toys for whipping up big rivers. They were particularly designed for Canterbury-style alluvial riverbeds, although South Westland and other areas offer ample opportunities for exploration. Big braided alluvial rivers are not usually suitable for fly-fishing and jetboats are primarily used as a means of transport to smaller tributaries and spring creeks.

More often than not fish remain unperturbed by a jetboat passing over them. Indeed, salmon anglers often claim that the experience perks the fish up and makes them easier to catch. We have powered over the top of rainbows and browns in Canterbury rivers in shallow runs, and then climbed out of the boat and hooked into them. So if you are fishing from shore and a jetboat blasts through, don't be totally disheartened because the fish should quieten down relatively quickly.

OPPOSITE: The scenic Waimaka-riri is a favourite river for jet-boaters.

The great thing about jetboats is that you can cover great amounts of terrain in short amounts of time and access locations that are difficult to reach on foot. There is also the thrill of speeding up the river, not to mention the chance to see great scenery.

POWERBOATS

Bigger power boats are especially good for accessing lake fisheries and tributary rivers and streams. Always make sure you are carrying more fuel than you expect to use. Be especially careful travelling after dark, because it is easy to become disorientated and run out of water. A stranded boat can be murder to relaunch!

It pays to practise good boat safety and to be particularly careful in stormy lake waters, as wind-generated swells can be more dangerous than the open sea. We've had some frightening trips on lakes and recommend that you never underestimate the power of nature.

SMALL BOATS

The trusty old aluminium dinghy. Campbell Whyte takes a break at the Windbag Stream, South Westland.

Small boats are useful in stillwater situations. They are handy for trolling, anchoring over weed beds, stalking cruising fish, or changing position around a lake. Trout are relatively unafraid of a slowly moving boat, so they make a good casting and viewing platform. We commonly use a 4-metre (13ft) aluminium dinghy and 15hp motor, with some old carpet and sacks on the bottom to reduce the metallic noises. Inflatables, fibreglass and wooden boats are similarly useful.

A great accessory for such boats is an electric positioning motor. These motors are silently powered by a marine battery that the fish never hear until it's too late. Such motors are far superior to oars and can be mounted on either the bow or the stern. They are great for trolling sinking fly-lines with streamers around lake edges and dropoffs during daylight hours and in the evening.

Backpacking a small inflatable boat into difficult areas like Lake Daniels makes it possible to enjoy some excellent fishing for rainbows.

RAFTING

Drifting down rivers and fishing from Mackenzie River drift boats is a popular activity in the western United States. In the US they are used to access large rivers and portions of rivers that are held in private ownership. We trust that the necessity to float down rivers as the only form of access will never become a reality here in New Zealand.

Small rafts are useful in a number of circumstances and locations in the South Island. They are mainly used on river beats and in tributary streams far away from roads. They are useful for crossing a large river in times of high flow, particularly when you want to reach the opposite bank that is inaccessible to other anglers. Fishing from the raft is not particularly successful, as New Zealand has lower fish densities, increased water clarity, and easily spooked fish.

One needs to be careful when rafting downriver to avoid upsetting other anglers; it is best to avoid popular rivers during the weekend and use the raft only on stretches of water not commonly fished. If you encounter other anglers, always try to stay on the far side of the river to be courteous. The other side is also good because you can't hear them swearing at you and they are less likely to hit you when they start throwing rocks!

Always wear lifejackets and be extremely careful. Learn how to handle your craft before attempting any major expeditions. Kids love rafting rivers and it's great fun even if you are not catching fish.

In summer some large rivers prove pleasant to fish by drifting to the tails of the pools, walking down and fishing the head of the pool below, then climbing back aboard and drifting downstream to the next likely location.

Using a mountain bike can be faster than walking …

MOUNTAIN BIKES

Mountain bikes are great for reaching rivers and alpine lakes via farm tracks and other rugged roads. Many farmers are now reluctant to allow motor vehicle access but will happily let you pedal over their property. There can be considerable time savings on bikes, and they allow anglers to skip over heavily fished or less likely water. Particularly arduous rides can be hard on your backside, however. It is difficult to smile when you're being cut in half.

A bike stand attached to the towball of your vehicle is handy for transporting the bike. It can be detached and locked in your car while you fish.

… but often there's no other way to get to those fish.

A good trick if you are fishing a large beat on a river paralleled by a good road is to drop your bike off upstream (where you intend to finish fishing) so that you can later ride back to your car. This can save hours of walking at the end of the day and allows you to spend more time fishing.

CHAPTER 10

ETIQUETTE, EXPECTATIONS, CONSERVATION

As many visitors to this country have discovered, despite their miniscule appearance on a world map the two main islands of New Zealand are quite substantial when you set off to drive around them. Both islands, but the South in particular, have hundreds, if not thousands of bodies of water that carry stocks of trout. The writers of this book have explored most of them, but to fish everything effectively could take several lifetimes. Despite this, the resource is finite, and increasing angling pressure is a fact of life. As one well-known guide sagely observed to us just last year, 'There are no secrets any more.' We tend to agree. While it would be nice to think that there are still some totally unfished streams left, in reality we doubt it. The search for the 'Holy Grail' goes on, of course, but increasing fishing pressure is an inevitable outcome of increasing physical and financial mobility.

This raises issues that were not even a consideration when some of us started fly-fishing in earnest more than a quarter of a century ago. Certainly there was always a flurry of activity at the start of the season each year, but after a month or two the rivers became largely the preserve of the serious anglers. Indeed, on some of the waters we fished we rarely encountered another angler. While the angling pressure in New Zealand is still far short of that existing in more populous countries, it is a factor worth considering and the potential for conflict exists.

There is a perceived problem for many anglers that their catch rates have declined because there are just too many people fishing South Island waters. Angling pressure *is* an important consideration in fisheries management, but we believe this has assumed too much importance in the minds of many people. The major factor in any fishery's viability is the quality of the habitat. If the habitat is of good quality and it is protected, then it will always hold reasonable fish numbers.

Good anglers realise that fisheries are a dynamic resource and that quality can fluctuate from year to year in response to environmental factors. And

OPPOSITE: Amazing, pristine waters are ripe for the fishing for those anglers who are prepared to explore remote valleys.

The search for the Holy Grail. Graeme Marshall decides the best plan of attack.

they recognise, with the advent of catch-and-release, that most fish are now returned to the wild and many fish are now able to elude capture altogether. Perhaps anglers concerned about falling catch rates have failed to increase their skill levels as fishing conditions have changed. Fishing pressure will definitely make fish more challenging to catch, but isn't that what fishing is all about? The South Island angling experience is still marvellous by world standards but it requires anglers to be continually learning new skills and be more innovative than before.

Another concern for many local anglers is increasing numbers of visiting anglers with professional guides. Such people should be reassured by the findings of Zane Mirfin's 1990 Masters thesis, 'Trout Fishing in Nelson: Management of a Recreational Resource' which surveyed local anglers and guides in the Nelson–Marlborough Fish and Game District. Despite this area being one of the most established fishing tourism areas in the South Island, total guided use was found to add up to less than 3 per cent of total fishery use. They might also acknowledge that tourism is vital to the New Zealand economy and it has placed an international value on many waterways, thus assisting in their preservation. Overseas ideas and technology have brought fisheries management out of the dark ages and have helped to preserve many New Zealand waters in perpetuity.

Anglers should be thankful that we have such a marvellous resource available to all. Anyone who believes the fishery is being thrashed should stop griping, get out on the water and just enjoy the fishing.

You're never too young to start fishing.

PROTOCOL AND ETIQUETTE ON THE WATER

The other angler could clearly see Zane fishing in the river as he tried to sneak into the water upstream. Guiltily he waded out 20m in front of Zane and started casting into the river. His body position looked awkward, as he glanced nervously back over his shoulder to assess the reaction.

'Hey!' Zane yelled at him. 'What the hell do you think you're doing?'

'I'm fishing for some trout I saw yesterday,' he spluttered.

'Don't you think it's a bit rude ruining the pool for me,' Zane reacted angrily. 'Just because you were down here yesterday doesn't mean you can barge in now and mess it up for me!'

To his credit, the guy got out of the water, walked down and apologised. After a brief chat Zane left the intruding angler and moved elsewhere. There wasn't enough water there for both of them, and there were plenty of other places to try.

Most people go fishing to enjoy ourselves, to avoid everyday hassles, and maybe catch a fish or two. The last thing anyone needs on a trout stream is conflict and aggression. Everyone should be considerate toward other people's rights, because there is plenty of water for everyone.

For years South Island anglers have enjoyed relatively uncrowded waters and few encounters with other anglers, except at commonly fished locations. Taking into account the low densities of fish, anglers may require many kilometres of river to have a productive fishing day. Many North Island and overseas anglers sometimes have trouble understanding the concept of giving an angler who was there first a suitable length of water to fish.

On the Tongariro River at Turangi, is not uncommon to find a dozen anglers in one pool when the spawning rainbows are running. British Columbian steelhead fishing can be shoulder to shoulder, and in many popular US rivers you may have to drive up and down the road looking for a vacant pool. Not so in the South Island. Once an angler is on the water you should assume that he or she is there for at least half a day and leave an appropriate amount of water.

There is no magic formula for deciding how much water to leave undisturbed for an already-resident angler. This comes through experience, time of day, local custom and knowing there are other opportunities in nearby waters. If you are unsure and it is possible to do so, then leave them more water than you think they can fish in a day and find another location.

Overseas anglers should take special care to leave other anglers plenty of water. Remember you are an ambassador for tourist anglers in decades to come, and good conduct in avoiding conflict with New Zealand anglers

Fortunately there aren't too many crowds like this on South Island rivers. Fishing for winter run rainbows, Tongariro River, North Island.

No, he wasn't pushed! Chris Gammons discovers that New Zealand rivers are often deceptively deep and swift.

You go upstream and I'll go down …

is strongly encouraged. Independent and unguided anglers from other countries should spread their angling effort over a number of waters. Camping on and fishing the same beat of water for a week in New Zealand is strongly discouraged. Besides, the constant pressure will make the fishing harder with each successive day.

Often it is possible to discuss options with anglers already present on the water and ascertain what they are hoping to do. Sometimes they are fishing only a few pools and may be happy for you to enter upstream at some predetermined location. Remember that the angler there first has the right of way and the latecomer should respect this.

Most fishermen are friendly enough and will appreciate your efforts to ascertain their intentions, with the result that some mutually satisfactory arrangement can be agreed. Always be friendly and courteous to your fellow anglers. Treat people as you would like to be treated yourself.

Some locations these days have reasonably heavy foot traffic and as an angler you can't realistically expect to have as much water to yourself as you might have had in the past. A fishing buddy, Cameron Reid, of Nelson, reckons you can expect to have the river to yourself for only half a day at the maximum in popular areas, especially at weekends. He thinks that if you get three or four hours of fishing alone, you've had a good morning and should be prepared to relocate to another part of the river if this is necessary. Careful anglers should be occasionally checking the shore for fresh bootprints, and if the fish appear to be sparse, then someone may be in front of you.

If somebody blatantly cuts in front of you this is known as 'jumping'. You should politely but firmly tell them what they have done wrong. Sometimes people deliberately get in front because they wish to fish a certain beat of water. Maybe they should have got out of bed earlier! Their posture expresses guilt and knowledge of their actions, and they spend most of their time looking back over their shoulder as if expecting retribution. Try not to get too upset as they are lesser people for their actions. You can't win an argument with such people but you should tell them about their poor manners. Most will be embarrassed and apologetic when the facts are pointed out to them.

Team work … and Luke and Dave Kelly have a great fish to show for it.

Unfortunately 'jumping' is becoming more common. It is also difficult sometimes to work out whether people are fishing in the river, and if so where they are, because they hide their vehicle, wear camo clothing, and fail to ask the local farmer for access permission. Keep an open mind; mistakes do happen, sometimes to otherwise well-intentioned anglers.

Generally if you are fishing waters near to the road, moving on to another location isn't too much of a problem. Often the worst situations occur in back-country rivers, where there is no chance of relocation when parties of anglers encounter each other. The only thing you can do in such situations is to sit down with them and work out a mutual agreement. If it turns into a race upriver then nobody wins. Perhaps one party can go upstream and the other downstream. If it is a small river, perhaps the parties can share the water and fish alternate pools. If the river is large, why not toss a coin for a side each, or fish some tributaries.

Take a break …

Whatever agreement you make, it should be fair to both parties, and you should abide by the verbal agreement that was made in good faith. Nothing angers fishermen more than someone agreeing to walk upstream through the bush to a certain (agreed) point, then reneging on the deal and starting fishing around the very next corner.

If someone is determined to race you upriver, let them go. Have a nap for a couple of hours then follow up behind them. Usually they will be moving so fast trying to stay ahead of you that they won't do very well – scaring fish and skimming past productive lies on both sides of the river. Fish have to eat to survive, and after a couple of hours, blind fishing into productive lies should produce successful hookups.

Please respect and appreciate your fellow anglers. With tolerance, co-operation and fair play, you should be able to resolve any potential problems in encounters with fellow anglers. We've made good friends in chance streamside encounters.

EXPECTATIONS

Not all NZ trout are huge!

There was a time when fly-fishers from other countries formed a mental image of New Zealand as the place where they could catch a trophy of a lifetime simply by casting a fly upon the nearest stream or lake. Travel agents did little to dispel this notion, and in many instances whipped up the fervour by publishing photos of huge trout in their promotional literature and implying that such fish were commonplace and easy to catch. It is pleasing to observe that the story is now told as it is, at least by reputable operators. Sure, the photos of big fish are still there – why not make capital out of them – but the other side of the coin needs to be shown too.

While the South Island may well be 'brown trout heaven' there are many factors that can leave the angler feeling that the actual experience was somewhat short of the dream. Let's be honest. Brown trout, and rainbows, too, in heavily fished waters, are rarely easy to catch. If you find the fish off guard or feeding so avidly that you could catch them with a broomstick for a rod and a feather duster with a hook attached for a fly, then savour that experience because it may be a long time before you are so fortunate again.

All anglers, no matter their level of expertise, experience occasional blanks. It may be that a howling gale blew downstream all day, making casting difficult if not impossible. The river may have suffered from a flood after a cloudburst in the mountains the night before. In this country weather and river conditions are probably the main determinant of angling success. It is quite common for a day to start out with perfect conditions that deteriorate with mind-boggling speed. New Zealand's South Island lies right in the path of the 'Roaring Forties', a belt of strong westerly winds that beset us in spring and summer every year. In the now all-too-common El Niño years an infernal wind can blow day and night, for days on end.

Sometimes, though, all appears stacked in the angler's favour – a sky of duck-egg blue, little wind and good visibility – but no fish! This scenario is most common on lowland rivers such as the Mataura and Motueka. Despite holding fish aplenty these waters sometimes demonstrate such a lack of trout life that you think you are casting over a fishless desert. The Mataura especially can seem totally devoid of fish when there is no hatch occurring. Guides dread such days. The owner of a US fishing lodge once observed to us that if any of his clients encountered a totally fishless day on his water he would sack the guide forthwith! There would be a lot of unemployed fishing guides in this country if that situation applied here. We have observed days when even the most expert of anglers struggle to tempt just one fish.

The wind – its direction and velocity – is often a major determinant of angling success.

In our experience perhaps the toughest time is mid-summer when water levels are getting down and a deep depression is approaching. We are convinced that trout are affected by a steep air pressure gradient. Evidence suggests that trout and other fish are able to detect significant changes in air pressure via their lateral lines and that they sense when a flood is on the way. It is possible, too, that the insects are able to detect a change in the weather and are able to delay their hatching. While lowering pressure is said to encourage a feeding binge in sea species we are adamant that browns seem edgy and reluctant to feed. Indeed, they are really hard to find. In a few instances we have actually observed fish moving to cover just before a flood.

Scott Mirfin enjoys a hot brew. It can be disappointing when the fishing is slow, but there are other pleasures to enjoy on a wilderness camping trip.

The phase of the moon is another significant factor. In our experience the time around full moon makes for less successful fishing, possibly because the fish are able to see their prey more easily at night, eliminating the necessity to feed so actively by day. If this were true, trout should be more easily caught at night, but this is definitely not the case – adding to the list of wonderful conundrums that make fly-fishing for trout such a superb sport.

Sometimes other factors are more important. In back-country areas we find that fish are nervy and extremely wary if subjected to constant angling pressure. It is certainly not wise to fish the same water two days running. While this is of little significance on the relatively heavily fished Motueka and Mataura rivers it is a very real factor on the Grey and the Oreti, for instance. Fish can become so spooked they are virtually uncatchable.

They're definitely there … but sometimes they're a bit hard to catch. *John Boyles*

When someone has travelled far and put a great deal of time and money into a 'dream' fishing trip it can be disappointing to experience tough fishing. Fly-fishers, though, are a phlegmatic and optimistic bunch in the main, and perseverance will normally pay dividends in the longer term. And there are other rewards to be savoured while fishing the South Island. The scenery alone is often nothing short of stunning, with rapidly changing light making for a photographer's paradise. The country is so neatly packaged that it is possible to move from a coastal environment to an alpine one in a very short distance, a 'plus' for the holiday-maker.

So what is an average day in the South Island like? In the superb photographic essay *Distant Waters*, which features the photographic images of well-known photographer R. Valentine Atkinson, Verlyn Klinkenborg describes a typical day thus: 'A good day might find an angler and guide spotting a dozen fish and catching five between 4 and 7 lbs.' This is probably pretty fair comment. Some days may see just a few fish to the net. Others, perhaps 20 or more. On a few occasions one or two of the fish landed may take the scale down to that magic figure in excess of 4.5kg (10 lb) – the stuff of dreams.

There is a saying that 'there are no bad fishing days – some are just better than others'. But even those occasional slow days can be fun.

CONSERVATION

While some may live for 12 to 15 years, trout are a relatively short-lived species by comparison with many saltwater fish. In this country a brown trout may achieve its maximum length and weight in just three years, and

A nice brownie on his way home.

that weight may be substantial. Obviously, no two catchments produce fish with exactly the same characteristics, and the average size of fish in a river will vary throughout the length of its waterway. Like many other creatures great and small, trout populations are dynamic and in a constant state of flux. We have observed significant variations in populations from season to season in the rivers we fish. They run in cycles. For a number of years a particular stream may hold a large population of relatively small fish. Then comes a year when the population may seem more balanced, with a wide range of sizes evident. Some of our back-country waters rarely seem to contain other than a very few, *very big* specimens, especially in the headwaters, quite contrary to the pattern existing in many other parts of the world.

Flood events are common in this country. The evidence of this is not difficult to find. Just cast a glance well above the normal flow zone and marvel at the size of the flood that placed pieces of driftwood high in that willow tree or an enormous log atop a boulder some 3–4m (10–13 feet) above the water surface. Such events must cause the demise of large numbers of fish, especially if they are caught unawares by a flash flood. Sometimes habitats may be severely damaged for years, after a massive slip causes rocks to smother sand on the riverbed. Eventually, though, habitats improve and as they do the fish return and set up residence there again.

Considering the viciousness of nature some would argue that the practice of catch-and-release achieves little. Maybe so, especially on larger waters where natural mortality far outweighs that which anglers could achieve even if they killed every fish caught. Browns are true survivors and are, in many instances, capable of handling a high degree of fishing pressure.

Brooks Walker demonstrates good release technique by gently cradling the fish and keeping it in the water.

However, on small tributary streams and in the back country, populations are often alarmingly small. To kill even a few fish is to damage the fishery significantly.

We are reminded of an instance on the Karamea River a few years ago, involving a group of spin fishers. Each day they went off independently and came back with a limit or near-limit of fish each, so much so that they were embarrassed by the quantity of fish they had to dispose of. Despite eating trout for every meal, and attempts to smoke some in the chimney of the hut they stayed in, there was inevitably a certain amount of waste. After the first day's carnage an attempt was made to explain the philosophy and practise of catch-and-release. While they listened politely they still could not conceive of the necessity for such action. They were catching plenty of fish, so there must be plenty there. Right? Wrong. They were damaging the

fish stocks. While no one is averse to eating a bit of trout on rare occasions, catch-and-release is somehow much more satisfying.

The principles of catch-and-release are really quite simple, but it is necessary to act calmly to give the fish the best chance of survival. Large, back-country trout frequently fight to total exhaustion which is all the more reason why they should be handled with extreme care to give them the greatest chance of survival. Always use the strongest possible tippet and exert pressure on the fish to bring it to the net quickly. If possible, remove the hook without handling the fish and while it is still in the water. If a photo is wanted, hold the fish out of the water for the briefest possible time and avoid touching the gills or squeezing the abdomen. Cradle rather than grip the fish and hold it into the current until it wants to move off of its own volition.

Despite claims to the contrary, catch-and-release does work. We have seen some fish caught and released a number of times with apparently no ill effects.

Fight fish hard to ensure an early release. Most anglers don't understand the full potential of a fly rod and exhaust and damage the trout unneccessarily.

Man-made influences on trout habitat are arguably the most destructive. Large-scale land clearance, forestry operations, cattle grazing on river berms and toxic discharges are the most potent threats to a healthy trout fishery. All anglers should be vigilant and report any breaches of the law or blatantly ignorant acts that could harm fish populations. Some anglers from overseas have remarked to us that New Zealand reminds them of what their own country was like 40 years ago, and they exhort us to fight to keep it that way by protecting our wonderful fishery by all means possible.

GUIDES

While most Kiwi anglers would no more consider hiring a guide than flying to the moon, the same does not apply to the increasing numbers of serious fly-fishers arriving from overseas destinations every year. Some of these, though, do try to do it alone. A typical example is worth recounting. Late one Sunday evening Graeme's phone rang and he found himself speaking to a young American who hastily enquired whether he was available the following day. Graeme replied in the affirmative and was then asked his daily guiding rate. The silence was deafening, and a quick conference was held with a third party, before he was asked if he would take on a half day for him and his friend. He agreed, and then the tale of woe was recounted. The two friends from Montana had travelled the length of the South Island and despite fishing hard from daylight till dark had nothing more than a few small fish to show for their efforts. They were nearing the

Intrepid guides taking a break …

Happiness is a bent rod! Experienced guides will add value to your fishing experience.

end of their New Zealand sojourn and were keen to make amends, even though they were on very tight budgets. They arranged to meet at a certain point on the Motueka River the next day. Graeme recounts the story thus.

I was really impressed with the physique of these two fresh-faced young men. They quickly told me they were fire jumpers from Montana, hence their tough, fit-looking appearance. As we discussed tactics and they told me a little of their Kiwi experience I cast a quick eye over their gear. It was top-of-the-line stuff, complete with grey lines and correct length leaders. The fly boxes were equally well equipped, so I selected a hare and copper and pheasant tail nymph combination for each, adjusted the indicators a little, and we were off up the edge of the shallow run under the willows. I noted a couple of quizzical glances to each other as I began searching the water right on the edge. I suggested that one of the pair stay with me while the other fished mid-stream. I soon realised that I was not dealing with novices. These guys could cast further and better than I ever could. As Ben fired out superb casts which just about reached the far bank, I stalked my way along the outside of the shadow cast by the lush, overhanging willows. I was soon rewarded by the sight of a fine fish nymphing confidently in a minor pocket in water less than 60cm deep. 'There you are Randy,' I remarked, trying to sound casual. 'Try for that one.'

'Which one, where?' replied my excited client. I quickly pinpointed the spot for Randy and an audible exhalation of breath prefaced his 'Wow, what a beauty.' Unlike some of his countrymen he had no difficulty seeing the fish once pointed out to him. The first cast was perfect. The fish sidled across, grabbed the lower nymph and raced off diagonally upstream. Randy played it expertly and we were soon all admiring a typically beautiful Motueka brownie of about 1.8kg.

The boys raved. It was now Ben's turn. Within a few metres I had another pinpointed and the performance was repeated. They were exultant. Sharing the fishing they took another four fish from the run until the water got too deep for us to proceed further. One fish was taken with a superb cast up under the willows with a dry fly. We moved to another spot and two more were landed, along with a few lost along the way. And then the half day, which had stretched somewhat, as I was enjoying myself so much, was over. We parted good friends. Subsequently we have corresponded and both assure me that they are coming back and will be hiring a guide for at least the first part of the trip next time.

For visitors, at least one day in the company of a guide is well nigh essential, if only to establish the methods used in that district. Of course there are guides and guides. Members of the New Zealand Professional Fishing Guides Association must have a reasonable track record to be accepted into that organisation and membership requires guides to adhere to a strict code of behaviour. The association's ethics committee will thoroughly investigate any complaints against its members. While word of mouth from satisfied customers is probably the best recommendation, it is possible to sort out a good, knowledgable guide in any area of the country by doing some homework. You could start by asking possible guides about the style of fishing they cater for; whether or not they carry Commercial Vehicle and Public Liability insurance and Occupational Safety and Health insurance, and whether they are the holders of current First Aid and CPR certificates. A potential guide will take time to respond courteously to any queries you may have, including the arranging of accommodation if necessary.

Fred Young is happy with his catch.

It is our considered opinion that the best guides in this country are those who have made guiding their prime source of income, who are usually independent operators or working within small networks. There are some good guides operating out of major fishing lodges, but be warned, superb though they may be, these luxury lodges cater for clients with very deep pockets. If that is your thing go for it, but be aware too that lodges do not offer the flexibility about meal times, for example, that independent guides operating from motels or homestays are able to offer. The latter are more prepared to travel on a daily basis if necessary, arrange camp-outs off the beaten track and generally provide a more comprehensive service.

CHAPTER 11

GENERAL INFORMATION FOR VISITORS

There are many excellent agents (and wholesalers) organising trips to New Zealand. They do a top job as they know the scene intimately and can take a lot of the hassle out of the trip by arranging guides, internal transfers, rental cars and accommodation. These organisations advertise at tackle shows, in magazines and via the Internet, as do many independent guides. Perhaps the best way to find out all you can about an organisation or operator is to speak to someone who has been there.

ACCOMMODATION

The accommodation and restaurant industry in New Zealand has recently undergone a revolution. Travellers these days are far more discerning and request larger rooms, ensuite bathrooms, unique architecture and design and, above all, services that make their journey interesting, relaxing and enjoyable. Restaurants featuring regional cuisine and New Zealand wines are found not only in the large urban areas but also throughout the countryside, much to the delight of the traveller. The wine-producing areas, including Nelson, Blenheim and Queenstown, offer exceptional food and wine in well-designed restaurants, bistros and cafés.

New Zealand has many unique small inns, lodges and hotels in all types of redesigned historic buildings, such as period homes refitted as bed and breakfasts, and homestays in renovated country homesteads. Hosts are friendly, knowledgable and helpful.

The days of the large luxury hotels and lodges are not gone, but they are undergoing changes to keep pace with newer accommodation that provides excellent service, food and wine in a well-designed environment.

Types of accommodation are categorised as follows:

Luxury hotels   NZ$200–1000

International and regional hotels found in the main cities and resorts. Meals not included in the rates quoted here.

Luxury lodges   NZ$350–1200

Exclusive accommodation in remote and scenic locations known for the excellence of their cuisine, service and atmosphere. Meals generally included.

Inns, unique hotels, small lodges   NZ$210–900

Located in cities and throughout the countryside. Known for the excellence of their service and atmosphere. Generally unique in architecture and design. Many with outstanding cuisine served in their own dining rooms or adjacent restaurants. Some meals included.

Motels and motor inns   NZ$90–200

Located throughout New Zealand. Most with cooking and laundry facilities. Meals not included.

Bed and breakfast, small hotels   NZ$100–250

Located throughout the country, some in unique or restored historic buildings. Breakfast included. Some provide dinner featuring regional cuisine and wines by prior arrangement.

Farmstay, countrystay, restored homesteads   NZ$140–200

These generally provide a room with private or ensuite facilities. Most include breakfast, with dinner by prior arrangement.

Hostels   NZ$20–60

Basic accommodation, often referred to as 'backpackers' lodges'. Communal facilities available. Bedding may be rented. Usually a three-night limit. Meals not included.

Motor camps, camping grounds and campsites   NZ$5–70

These offer spaces for tents, caravans (trailers), and campervans. Electricity provided. Bathroom, showers, cooking facilities and laundry are centrally located. Bare cabins offer beds (no linen – bring your own sheets and towels), while flats (small apartments) offer equipped kitchens and beds with linen.

Back country Hilton. Huts such as these provide welcome refuge for wet and tired anglers at the end of a long day. They're very basic accommodation, available to all on a first-come, first-served basis.

Country lodges provide excellent atmosphere, cuisine and service. *Doc Ross*

BANKING

During the week, banks are open from 9.00am to 4.30pm. Automatic teller machines (ATMs) are available and can be used with credit cards. It is a

Many couples enjoy fishing together and sharing each other's success.

good idea to have a PIN number encoded onto your card for security reasons. Major credit cards are accepted throughout New Zealand. Visa and Mastercard are most common, with American Express and Diners cards not being accepted by some smaller businesses. Many bed and breakfast (B&B) and homestay operations also accept Visa and Mastercard, although some accept only cash, travellers cheques, or a NZ bank cheque. If in doubt, always ask beforehand to clarify the situation.

It pays to carry enough money for immediate expenses because your schedule will not always match the banking hours and many rural areas have no banking facilities.

BUSINESS HOURS

Offices and businesses are open weekdays from about 8.30am to 5pm. Stores and shops are usually open from 9am to 5.30pm, with weekend shopping in the larger centres. Supermarkets and small convenience stores, called dairies, have longer hours and are generally open on weekends. There is very little 24-hour service and on public holidays many shops and other services will be closed.

In remote areas, such as in parts of the West Coast, it is often a long way between banks, grocery stores and gas stations. Make it a habit to fill your petrol tank when you go past a station.

Another magnificent brown trout!

CURRENCY

The New Zealand dollar ($NZ) is divided into 100 cents. Coins are 5c, 10c, 20c, 50c, $1 and $2. Notes are $5, $10, $20, $50 and $100. Currency exchange is available at banks and the Auckland, Wellington, Christchurch and Queenstown airports.

DRIVING: LEFT-HAND DRIVE

In New Zealand driving is on the left-hand side of the road. There are increasing numbers of road accidents involving tourists who were driving on the wrong side of the road. Overseas drivers should remember that they will be driving on the opposite side of the road in a right-hand drive vehicle. Familiarise yourself with the typical road signs, especially signs for one-lane bridges. Be alert, drive carefully and defensively. Many New Zealand roads are narrow, often winding and, in the back country, unsealed. Give yourself plenty of time to reach your destination and avoid driving after dark on unfamiliar roads. Always be aware of other drivers on the road and be especially careful overtaking other vehicles.

Rob and Jana Bowler with Gunnar
Westrin on the shores of Lake Rotoiti.
Leif Milling

The official New Zealand guide to traffic rules and traffic safety is a well-illustrated, easy-to-read book called *The Road Code*.

ELECTRICAL SUPPLY

New Zealand operates on AC electricity at 230/240 volts, 50 hertz, the same as Australia, but the plugs are different. There is usually a 110-volt, 20-watt outlet in hotels and motels for razors. A set of adaptor plugs and converter is handy to have for a razor, hairdrier or laptop computer. Adaptor plugs are available at international airport shops and at major city electrical stores.

HEALTH SERVICES

New Zealand offers health facilities in public and private hospitals and clinics, with an excellent standard of care. Check the front pages of the local telephone directory for doctors and other medical services. The term 'chemist' is used instead of 'drugstore' but it has most of the same items as well as being a pharmacy. Travellers should have their own comprehensive travel and health insurance before entering New Zealand.

POSTAL SERVICES

Post Shops, stationery shops and bookshops sell stamps, stationery and postcards. Use the Fast Post stickers and rates for airmail to the USA and Europe. It generally takes seven to ten days to reach the USA.

PUBLIC HOLIDAYS AND SCHOOL HOLIDAYS

Beside the usual holidays of the Christian calendar such as Christmas Day, Good Friday and Easter Monday, New Zealanders observe Boxing Day (January 26), New Year's Day, Waitangi Day (February 6), Anzac Day (April 25) and Labour Day (third Monday in October). As well there is a number of provincial anniversary days throughout the year. Services are generally still available throughout the country on most of these days, apart, possibly, from on Christmas Day, Good Friday and the morning of Anzac Day.

School holidays vary throughout the country, but most schools are closed for the last two weeks of December and the whole of January, the major period for family holidays and a time to avoid popular beach and lakeside resorts if you dislike crowds. There are also three periods of two to three weeks each at regular intervals throughout the year when schools are closed.

RESTAURANTS AND GROCERY SHOPPING

Large cities have many excellent restaurants to select from, with a variety of food styles. Out in the country, small rural towns may only have a pub with a restaurant that serves lunch occasionally and dinner only on certain nights. Generally tea rooms serve breakfast and lunch. Hosts at bed and

breakfast and homestay residences usually offer dinner for an extra charge if you arrange it ahead of time.

So many roads, so many rivers.
Leif Milling

Grocery stores, especially in larger towns, offer a good variety of food stuffs. Fresh fruit and vegetables can be bought from roadside stalls throughout the South Island. Many areas offer the opportunity to pick your own fruit and berries over the summer and autumn months for minimal cost. Vineyards are good value for excellent New Zealand wines.

SHOPPING

Department stores, boutiques and craft shops offering local handcrafted items and clothes are located throughout the South Island. Generally, the best value for woollen sweaters and handcrafted items is found in small towns and rural country areas.

TAXES

A tax of 12.5 per cent (Goods and Services Tax or GST) applies to all goods and services in New Zealand including food, transport, guiding, etc. All prices displayed are tax inclusive (it's a legal requirement), so there should be no unpleasant surprises.

TELEPHONE SERVICES

Most Telecom-provided public phones are now operated by credit-card-sized phone cards available from bookstores, news-stands, postal outlets, and 24-hour petrol stations. You can select the amount you want to spend on the card when purchasing. Telecom accepts credit card payments for national and international calls through the operator. Cellular phone service is a way of life for many New Zealanders. Cells cover most of both the North and South Islands, and service is increasing in remote areas. Ask your current cellular telephone provider what service is available to you. It may be as simple as programming an international roaming number.

Important phone numbers

Emergency	111
Local Operator	010
International operator	0170
International directory assistance	0172

The access code for dialling direct overseas from New Zealand is 00. Then dial the country code (which for the USA is 1) before the area code.

'Collect' and credit card calls direct through a USA operator

USA (AT&T)	000911	Pacific	20
USA (MCI)	000912	Alaska	20–22
USA (Sprint)	000999	Hawaii	22

TIME DIFFERENCE

Daylight Saving Time in New Zealand starts on the first Sunday in October and ends on the third Sunday in March; clocks are set an hour forward during this time. The following table is for hours behind New Zealand time (Standard Time) in the USA:

Eastern	17
Central	18
Mountain	19

An easy way to remember is that when you are in New Zealand you are a day ahead of the USA and 3–5 hours behind. For example, if it is Saturday in New Zealand at 7.00am, then it is Friday in the USA, Pacific time, between 10.00am and noon, depending on Daylight Saving Time.

TIPPING AND SERVICE CHARGES

Tips and gratuities are not generally expected for service, including restaurant and bar service, although this may not be true of the more expensive international hotels. If you wish to leave a tip in gratitude for outstanding service this is acceptable, although not expected. No service charges are added to hotel or restaurant accounts.

WATER SUPPLY

Back-country rivers and lakes may contain giardia, so you should boil or treat water before drinking. We like to use portable pump-operated water purifiers. City water as well as hotel and motel tap water is fresh and safe to drink. New Zealand is fortunate in having relatively pure river water by world standards. Please respect this, and bury toilet wastes well away from water sources.

For more detailed information about New Zealand, a good place to look is on the Internet. There are dozens of web sites which, between them, will tell you everything you need to know.

Water purifying pumps are recommended on many South Island rivers these days.

FURTHER READING

SOUTH ISLAND MAPS

Maps for the districts outlined in Chapter 3 are helpful and readily available. Road maps produced by a number of companies provide distance charts, major city and town maps, and regional road maps. The New Zealand Automobile Association is well worth joining for many reasons and has a number of excellent publications available for travelling motorists. Tourist information offices are liberally scattered around the South Island and are easily located by travellers.

For a more detailed source of maps, especially rivers and lakes, Reeds *New Zealand Atlas*, published in association with the Department of Survey and Land Information (DOSLI), is perfect for the inquisitive angler. Since its first publication this atlas has probably led to the investigation and persecution of more trout streams than any other publication. Every good New Zealand trout angler we know owns one.

For more accurate topographical information, maps in the 1:50000 scale are better. They are available in various bookstores and Department of Conservation offices, or can be ordered direct from the Infomap Centre, Private Bag 903, Upper Hutt, Wellington.

GUIDE BOOKS

For more detailed description of the rivers, lakes, and streams of the South Island there are a number of guide books. The best will be described and listed first.

South Island Trout Fishing Guide by John Kent (Octopus Publishing). This volume and its companion *North Island Trout Fishing Guide* are the best and most complete set of guidebooks.

Trout Fishing in Southland New Zealand (Southland Fish and Game Council). An excellent review of Southland waters.

The Guide to Trout Fishing in Otago edited and revised by Brian Turner (Otago Fish and Game Council). A detailed and well-written guide to the waters of Otago.

OPPOSITE: A magical spot in the West Coast rainforest – with a very optimistic fisherman.

World capital of brown trout fishing …
Leif Milling

Trout Fishing: A Guide to New Zealand's South Island by Tony Busch (David Bateman Ltd, 1994, 1999). A useful guide to the more accessible South Island rivers and lakes. Access points are clearly described. Fishing advice is of lesser quality.

RECOMMENDED NEW ZEALAND TROUT FISHING BOOKS

Images of Silver: A Guide to Backcountry Fishing by Les Hill and Graeme Marshall (Halcyon Press, 1993). A hardcover book with superb back-country photographs and fine text on back-country fishing techniques.

Stalking Trout: A Serious Fisherman's Guide by Les Hill and Graeme Marshall (Halcyon Press, 1985, 1989). A detailed account of how to spot and stalk trout. The best 'how-to' book on the subject.

Trout Stream Insects of New Zealand: How to Imitate and Use Them by Norman Marsh (Millwood Press, 1983). One of the best all-time New Zealand angling books. Concentrates on bugs and imitations but later chapters on fishing experiences are classic beyond description.

Choose the Right Fly by Keith Draper (Shoal Bay Press, 1997). A small, inexpensive but invaluable guide to trout stream insects and their imitations.

Stalking Stillwaters by Les Hill, (Halcyon, 1997). The most comprehensive book on fishing New Zealand's stillwaters.

Fly Fishing New Zealand's South Island by Rob and Jana Bowler (Boar's Head Press, 1995). Overview of South Island regions, rivers, techniques and essential travel information.

INSTRUCTIONAL BOOKS

USA writers lead the world in instructional fishing texts and we strongly recommend the following books, which New Zealand bookshops should be able to trace for New Zealand residents.

Lake Fishing with a Fly, by Ron Cordes and Randall Kaufmann (Frank Amato Publications, 1984). This is the best book on fishing stillwaters and is directly applicable to fishing in New Zealand.

Reading Trout Streams, by Tom Rosenbauer (Nick Lyons Books, 1988). A wonderful book detailing the intricacies of understanding moving trout water. Will pay dividends by increasing your catch rate.

Dry Fly Fishing and *Nymph Fishing*, by Dave Hughes (Frank Amato Publications, 1994, 1995). Excellent books for beginners and intermediate anglers, describing different techniques and angling situations in a precise manner. Highly recommended.

ABOUT THE AUTHORS

ZANE MIRFIN

Zane Mirfin is a professional fly fishing guide based out of St Arnaud on the shores of Lake Rotoiti in Nelson Lakes National Park. Zane has BSc and MA degrees, with his 1990 Masters thesis being titled 'Trout Fishing in Nelson: Management of a Recreational Resource'. Zane has fished and hunted throughout the South Island and continues to enjoy exploring and photographing this world class resource. He has fished extensively overseas in such faraway locations as Sweden, USA, British Columbia and Christmas Island, with four northern summers spent guiding in Colorado.

Zane is also a real estate professional specialising in rural, recreation and li̇ʳ   ᵏ him out on the following websites:

New Zealand
Travel & Fly Fishing

BrownTroutHeaven.com   ᵓm

The Ultimate Resource
800-953-9732

GRAEME MARSHALL

Former teacher and professional trout fishing guide, Graeme Marshall is well known to New Zealand outdoor sportsmen through his 'Sporting Scene' column in *Rod & Rifle* magazine. He has collaborated with Les Hill on the highly successful books *Stalking Trout*, *Catching Trout*, and *Images of Silver*.

Graeme lives at Ngatimoti, close to the Motueka river. He is vitally interested in many forms of fishing and hunting. Other interests include wetland restoration and working on the four-hectare property that he and his wife Raewyn own. The couple has two children, Alistair and Rhonda, who are currently involved in tertiary studies.

ROB BOWLER and JANA BOWLER

Rob Bowler has had a passion for fly-fishing since he grew up fishing in the ponds, rivers and saltwater bays of New England. He first visited New Zealand in 1978 as a visiting scholar attending the University of Canterbury where he studied and produced an extensive research document on the early history of New Zealand for the University of California. He did take time out from his studies to fly-fish many of the waters of both the North and South Islands and he has written a number of magazine articles on New Zealand fly-fishing over the last 20 years.

Jana Bowler, an avid fly-fisher, enjoys exploring rivers, lakes and streams with Rob in search of large, challenging brown trout. She holds the distinction of being the only woman ever awarded the Southland Fly Fishing Club President's Cup for the largest brown trout of the season. She is an experienced fly-tyer, a photographer and she has been a designer for commercial architecture for over 30 years.

Rob and Jana's home and office in Oregon USA overlooks the North Umpqua River, famous for its fly-fishing for summer and autumn steelhead. They travel to New Zealand every year and it was their intimate knowledge and love for the country that influenced the founding of New Zealand Itineraries, a travel consulting service which organises itineraries for visits to both the North and South Islands.

Rob and Jana can be contacted in the USA at 1-800-953-9732 or by writing to them at 344 Smith Springs Lane, Idleyld Park, Oregon 97447. In addition, you can visit their website at www.nicefish.co.nz for information about travel and fly-fishing in New Zealand.

Jana Bowler, left, and Rob Bowler, each with a fine Southland brown trout. *Rob Bowler (left) and Mac McGee*